FISCHIPS

A N/
TREASURE

CELEBRATING 150 YEARS OF BRITAIN'S FAVOURITE DISH

celebrating
150
years of
FISH'N'CHIPS
1860 - 2010
still the Nation's favourite!

MARK
PETROU

Acknowledgements

Anyone who knows me knows the score. They know how passionate I am about fish and chips and they also know that what I don't know about fish and chips isn't worth knowing. What I have committed to print represents about a third of what I originally wrote for this book. I have been so strict about it because I really wanted to offer to the industry I work in something to give to the general public, that would both amuse and educate. I had no agenda at all to impress anyone. I'm not the kind of person to go all anorak and commit all of my knowledge to print for the sake of it.

I conceived the idea for this book to serve as a tool for the frier to bring his customers up to speed. This book has a job to do and I've pitched it right down the middle on purpose. It is written with just enough technical stuff to interest people in fish and chips but not so much that it becomes like a trip to the dentist to read. It is designed to serve as a window for our customers to look through into the world of the frying trade and hopefully "take away" the reality that actually fish and chips is far too cheap for what it is, much better for you than you actually realise and something that our nation can really truly be proud of.

There're loads of people I need to thank. Rather than accept an Oscar, I will list them in no particular order and without anecdote. Kelvin Baines, Wendy Durham, Arthur Parrington, Ian "ha ha haggis" Watson, Marcus French, Jean and Peter Ritson, Fred Capel, Bill and Jean Shaw, Richard Ord, Brent and Anne Watson, Stelios Theocharous, Briar and Kelvin Lee, Robert Furey, Luca Senatore, Hannah Ballbag Shillito, Ian Kilby, Peter Petrou, My Friends, Family, Staff and my wife Clare Petrou. I also need to recognize contributions from Seafish, the National Federation of Fish Friers, the publication "The Fish Frier and His Trade" and finally the internet.

Any resemblance to any previously published work is purely coincidental – these are all my own words but it can only be a matter of time before someone puts their words in the same order as someone else without actually knowing it. Much of the content is derived from horse's mouth interviews, personal experience and direct research. When appropriate, I have sought to obtain a personal top five favourite list of chip shops from a contributor who was willing to share it. These people are the real scholars of the fish and chip trade (class of 2010) and they know what they are talking about.

So here is my book. I am hoping to cause a stir - without offence. You will almost certainly disagree with many of my comments and conclusions. This is good. It means that there is going to be a wave of counter claims, heated debate and more books on this fascinating subject. This pleases me a lot. This book is not a typical formula book that has a beginning, middle and end. It should offer some satisfaction, though, and includes a chapter of already published satire that I have contributed to the trade over the past year or so in the pages of Fish & Chips and Fast Food magazine. It's included because again I feel it captures my mood about many relevant subjects connected to the trade right now.

The only books before mine on the subject didn't really challenge the spectator at all – they were devised to document and pontificate and not to entertain and speculate. My book is meant to be part lovers' guide, as well as telling an important story from the point where the last decent book on the subject left off. The reason I'm determined to tell it is because the trade is fed up with an out of date image that needs replacing.

Read this book and spread the word. My contribution is left open for absolutely anyone to improve upon. Don't tell me next time you see me what I've got wrong factually though – unless I've asked you for your opinion.

If you've picked this book up and fingered through it before making your purchase, I hate you.

Enjoy my story...

Mark Petrou

FOREWORD

Fish and chips has involved a pretty steep learning curve for me since I took on the editorship of one of the sector's leading trade magazines, Fish & Chips and Fast Food, some four and a half years ago. Having spent a number of years in PR and journalism in a variety of different industries ranging from heavy engineering to the gift and jewellery trade, fish and chips was also an utter revelation.

Never before had I come across an industry where the guiding light was individual passion for the job in hand. From the smallest to the largest, all successful fish and chip businesses are driven by a passionate commitment to offer the best. The best food, the best service, the best hygiene, the best sustainable practices - each is inextricably linked, building into a whole which transforms the humble takeaway from an easy option at the end of a busy day to a really delightful eating experience.

I've had - and still have - many mentors who have guided my thirst for knowledge of this - the oldest takeway trade in the country - and Mark Petrou has been one of the most patient and helpful teachers you could imagine. It's not all been one way - since Mark began writing regularly for FCFF in 2007 I have used my professional experience to guide his pen and improve his powers of expression, just as he has steered my knowledge of the many ramifications of his trade. The result of that collaboration is this book, penned straight from Mark's heart, in the inimitable style which he has made his own. Long planned, and now delivered for the enjoyment of the trade and its many customers.

Media distortion

One of the biggest problems experienced by the fish and chip sector is that there is no coherent representative body which talks to their customers. Virtually every other high street retail business you can think of has consumer oriented media serving its interests. Want a camera? Need the best groceries? After a new bike? Or new camping equipment? Desperate for a new computer or printer? Need a new TV? You name it, there will be a consumer-oriented magazine on the shelves of W H Smith which is dedicated to that particular product and reviews the market, describes advances in the sector and generally informs and reassures customers.

But if you want to discover which is the freshest/healthiest/tastiest/ most cost-effective takeaway for your family? Zilch. Nada. Nil. Only the red-top media are interested in what is probably the largest collective retail business in the UK - the high street takeaway trade. And because it forms just a tiny part of their overall brief, their knowledge is woefully poor, influenced by big advertising spends and generally restricted to the latest popular scare story. With the result that when the general public DOES get to read in the media about fast food, the information is weak, slanted, poorly researched and often just plain wrong.

The media treatment of fish and chips is a paramount example of the dissemination of inaccurate and deeply misleading information.

We have been told only recently that local councils are insisting that fish and chip shops must cut their chips larger to lower their fat content and reduce the obesity problem. Reading this book will tell you that some chippies are already doing this, but even so, the inference that fish and chips is in in some way responsible for the present "obesity crisis" is deeply misleading. Do the skinny fries served in the burger chains and Kentucky Fried Chicken have nothing to do with it? And what about the fat content of the average cheese-laden pizza? Or the oil in a chicken tikka masala? Or the calorific content of even a Subway sandwich?

Last year, excessive litter was laid at the door of fish and chips, with a series of posters depicting youngsters with pig snouts and tails creating litter mountains outside fish and chip shops. The report on which this was based did in fact identify packaging from a leading burger chain as the worst offender - but it was fish and chips that took the rap.

When the tight quota restrictions were applied to cod in the North Sea four years ago because of overfishing, fish and chips was again blamed for pillaging the North Sea and destroying the cod stocks, not to mention UK fishermen's livelihoods. Nothing could be further from the truth. The majority (over 85% according to the Frozen at Sea Fillets Association) of cod and haddock served in the UK's fish and chip shops comes (and has done for years!) from certified sustainable fisheries in Arctic waters far to the north, and is gutted, filleted and frozen at sea within 2-4 hours of being caught. The nearest it gets to the North Sea is being shipped through it to one of the East Coast ports, where it arrives fresher than fresh.

And in spite of numerous laboratory tests by Seafish and others, which categorically prove that fish and chips - with its pure natural ingredients - is the lowest-fat popular high street takeway, fish and chips is repeatedly described by the media as being fat-ridden, unhealthy and bad for you, and this message is rammed home to the general public on every conceivable occasion.

Time for the truth

This book, which dispels the popular myths about fish and chips and tells it like it is, is targeted not only at the trade, but at the man in the street.

Should the man in the street only get as far as this foreword, he will learn that fish and chips has but five ingredients, all from natural sources: fish, potatoes, water, flour and frying medium. He will discover that fish and chips is invariably freshly produced from scratch, every day, immediately before being fried and served. Fresh potatoes are peeled and chipped; fish is cut into appropriately sized portions; batter is freshly made. He will learn that due to advances in frying equipment and techniques, the average portion of fish and chips nationwide contains only 9.4g of fat per 100g - significantly and sometimes massively less than most high street takeaways. Add a portion of mushy peas, and the fat count drops to well under 6g per 100g, as recently proved by Richard Ord of Colmans of South Shields in independent public analyst tests. He will also find that fish and chips are not responsible for a cod-free North Sea, the destruction of orang-utan natural habitats, nor for the cutting down of the rainforests. He will learn that even at today's prices, fish and chips is still an incredibly inexpensive way to sustain his family with good, honest food, honestly prepared by experts in their field.

Above all, he will learn that the media lie to him, mislead him and have very little interest in presenting the truth. As the famous quote goes, "Why let the facts stand in the way of a good horror story?"

I applaud Mark's efforts in this book to give a factual account of fish and chips. How it started. Where it probably began. How it has evolved through the last 150 years and two World Wars to become the iconic dish it is today, whilst still offering superlative value for money compared with other high street offerings. I'd encourage every fish frier in the UK to buy this book for themselves, and to buy a healthy stock for onward distribution to their customers.

After all, a better informed customer is a better customer. And that's what everyone wants, isn't it?

Wendy Durham
Editor
Fish & Chips and Fast Food Magazine

CONTENTS

CHAPTER ONE: THE DISH ITSELF...

Fish and chips fried to perfection cannot be beaten. And whenever a regional debate takes place about our national treasure, it will usually result in fisticuffs. For every man, woman and child there is a conflicting opinion about what makes the perfect fish supper and where the best fish and chip shop in the land is situated. In this book you will get just one man's opinion – mine. You are in safe hands, though, because I am an expert on the deep fried ambrosia. In this book I will tell you exactly where the best fish and chips can be found; I will take you on a journey from the industry's humble beginnings right up to its place as one of the cornerstones of national pride and beyond. I hope that by the end of this book you can accept that I have earned the right to call myself an expert on this subject...

There's something quite magical that happens whenever the words fish and chips are uttered...

This book celebrates two raw materials that are harvested from nature and then simply cleaned, cut and cooked. Trusty spuds grown in our very own neighbours' soil and free range fish taken from the ocean by the bravest of brothers who enter a hostile Arctic environment never meant to support mankind even in the calmest of weathers.

No matter what part of the country you are from, there is an independent retailer in your high street who has tailored his fried fish operation to suit your needs. There is not a more honest meal out there today that can boast the same virtues or hold the same place in our nation's heart.

Recent surveys have placed fish and chips at number one in the search to find the nation's favourite smell and in another poll it finished in top spot yet again as a true British Icon above Her Majesty The Queen, The Beatles and Princess Diana .

Tradition dictates that it should be reproduced in beef dripping – Londoners will have none of that. For the Scots it must be haddock and in Lancaster they reckon they were the start of it all. I am afraid if you are looking for answers, I am merely a servant of my craft who is desperate to share my version of the truth. Another cat amongst the pigeons, if you like, but the fact remains that my findings and this account stand up as well as anybody else's before me. With an image firmly cemented in the past, it is my genuine desire to reach out in a forward motion and give fish and chips the recognition it needs to be around for another 150 years.

There's something quite magical that happens whenever the words fish and chips are uttered. Whether you're in the mood or not, young or old, rich or poor, it's a meal that crosses all social barriers and its mandate from the very start has always been to provide affordable food for the masses. Nearly 300 million portions are sold every year in the UK from 11,000 shops. It's an industry that employs over 60,000 people, consumes more than 10% of our country's whole potato crop and takes £1.00 out of every £100.00 spent on food in the UK every single day. Not only that, the dish itself contains around 40% less fat than a kebab, burger and fries, pizza, Chinese or Indian meal.

Don't get me started about cod stocks in the North Sea, fishing wars, the definitive batter recipe, the best shop in the UK or why fish and chips isn't wrapped in newspaper any more – I'll get to all of those things as you turn the pages. I need to slow down a bit and do this thing properly.

Let me start with the basic raw materials....

Ocean wild

There are around 21,000 types of fish and shellfish in the world. There are over 100 different species available for human consumption anywhere in the UK today and literally thousands of different recipes and ways to eat them. In this book, though, we will concentrate on the first species of fish to be battered, the most popular fish on menus in

shops of today and the ones to look out for tomorrow.

The first fish to be battered and fried in the UK was probably a flatfish called a dab. The British Isles are fortunate enough to be surrounded by a fantastic variety of flatfish who start life typical in shape to most fish and as they mature, their eyes move round to either their left side or their right so that they have better vision when lying on the sea bed. Most species have a dark side (where their eyes are) and a white side which provides a natural camouflage from predators when viewed from either above or below (the sea bed being dark and view to the surface being light.) More commonly known types of flat fish that are battered and fried include plaice and Dover sole and there are many others including halibut, turbot and lemon sole.

Dabs were used by early fish friers as they were cheap, readily available and often overlooked at market in favour of larger species. When fried they have a similar taste and texture to plaice and still remain a good buy, as they have never achieved the same recognition as their more famous cousins. Dover sole is often described as the King of Soles. Considered to be quite a posh fish in comparison to plaice in respect of its modern position on UK menus, it is lovely when fried in batter and it benefits from a day or two's rest after catching in order to soften and sweeten.

Plaice is the third most popular fish sold in UK fish and chip shops today. It is available all year round fresh in the UK but the best time is in the summer months. I always recommend using plaice as quickly as possible when it is fresh to get the very best flavour from it which is delicate and sweet. Most fish and chip shops in the UK use IQF (individually quick frozen) fillets of plaice, which - once defrosted - provides them with year round consistency and locks in the freshness without compromising on quality. Fish freezes as well as most vegetables do and the process is performed in two main ways. IQF involves placing a thin glaze of water over the fillet prior to freezing to protect the flesh. This simply melts away when defrosted to expose the perfectly preserved fish. This practice is more commonly carried out once fish has been landed back on shore. The other way is for fish to be block frozen at sea. This method involves the processing of fish from whole fish to fillet as close to catching as possible – usually in under 2 hours. The fillets are then frozen on the boat in block form with layers of protective plastic between fillets to preserve the flesh and make them easy to separate. It

is then transported back to shore frozen, distributed frozen and then defrosted prior to cooking, resulting in an almost fresher than fresh product, as if it came straight from the ocean.

Cod could be a whole chapter all by itself. The amount of misinformation reported by the media relating to the most popular fish in the UK almost defies logic. They would have you believe that it has been almost fished to extinction. The truth is quite different and most of the stories only relate to North Sea stocks in any case – which only represent about 4% of the global cod supply. In other waters similar to the North Sea, measures are in place to ensure cod stocks are monitored and not over fished. 95% of British fish and chip shops source their cod responsibly – from sustainable stocks further north in Norwegian, Icelandic and Faroese waters and have done so for decades.

Cod is a lovely fish which never goes out of fashion. Available all year round – fresh or frozen - the English have always had a love affair with cod for its subtle flavour and very white flesh. It has many close relatives that have only slightly different characteristics and yet they have never seemed to attract the following they truly deserve. A lot of hard work has been put in by Seafish and in more recent times the large supermarket chains and many tree hugging environ "mental" types to try and attract the buying public away from cod because of the bad press it has unjustifiably received. Most media stories relating to cod have negative spin on them. Cod stocks are at a twenty year high but who wants to report that – it'd be like Heat magazine reporting that every celebrity marriage is intact!

Seafish is a non-departmental Government Authority which is funded by a levy on all seafood brought into the UK. Seafish is responsible for regulating and monitoring all things fishy, from research, catching and quotas to training, marketing and the consumption of seafood. Their involvement in the whole seafood supply chain serves all interested parties including the daily catch itself and helps to provide all the necessary information required to effectively introduce responsible practices for a sustainable approach to this massively important industry.

Their expertise has helped to combat the misinformation about over fishing and ensure that appropriate measures have been put in place to protect the long term future for both species of seafood and human livelihoods alike. Their website www.seafish.org is well worth a visit for any seafood lover whether you are in the trade or just want a great recipe idea.

Haddock   *Image courtesy NOAA*

Seafish have a much more balanced and transparent agenda when it comes to promoting other lesser known but more plentiful and sustainable species of seafood because it is celebrating and promoting an entire industry rather than trying to profit from or destroy it. You should be able to enjoy cod for years to come without feeling guilty as long as you ask whether it has been sourced responsibly or not. Any good purveyor should be able to confirm this but at the same time, don't be afraid to go off piste and sample some of the lesser known plentiful and available local seafood – you may well find one that ticks all your boxes for a fraction of the price than the more popular species command.

Haddock fits in at number two in the Fish and Chip Lovers' top three fish behind cod and ahead of plaice. It is a member of the cod family and the only one to have any real following of its own in the UK. It does not grow as big as cod and is not quite as robust but it does have a sweet taste and is more popular the further north you travel, taking the top spot from cod in Scotland.

These regional preferences go back to before both World Wars and the introduction of the British rail network. When fish was caught daily and collected from the docks, you sold the local fish. Now transporting

Frozen pollock fillets

goods around the UK is similar to time travel – but the regional favourites have remained intact almost like a stain on each community passed from father to son.

Lesser known cousins but well worthy of a mention are coley and hake which are good for frying but pollock (the most popular fish in France) which is slightly grey compared to cod and with less resistance in texture, has been made more popular in recent times by celebrity chefs who have made it trendy - in particular Gordon Ramsay. Pollock is likely to develop even more of a following as consumers with a conscience listen to the news and change their eating habits from cod.

Not one of these fish will break the bank compared to cod and are strongly recommended as they are not likely to take even the most cautious eater out of their comfort zone. They have delicate flavours and similar textures to the more popular species. Of course there are so many more terrific species of fish that will fry, but for whatever reason, be it yield, price or year round availability, they are likely to remain on restaurant or domestic menus rather than appearing in the form of a fish and chip supper.

I am a strong advocate of leaving certain jobs up to professionals to perform. With so many fires in the home being caused by chip pans and having seen how quickly they can get out of hand, I would always, always, always recommend buying your fish and chips from your local favourite chippy. I for one - and I'm sure many other proprietors - will either source a particular species for you or if you buy your own and take it into the shop, will be happy to batter and fry it for you for a small charge – as long as you buy some chips to go with it.

One potato, two potato...

When we think of the humble spud there are several names that automatically spring to mind. King Edward, Maris Bard, Cara and the ultimate king of frying potatoes – Maris Piper. There are about 450 varieties grown in the UK - of which 80 varieties are grown commercially and only one main annual crop of potatoes is harvested each year here. The harvest runs from June to October every year and the early varieties that I tend to fry are Maris Bard and Premier. Premier is slightly yellow in colour compared to Bard, but they both display similar characteristics in that they fry crisp and taste extremely sweet and yummy but soon lose

their crispness and succumb to a clumpy orgy in the chip box. That makes serving them up a devil but eating them with a little throw away fork a real treat.

Potatoes are often described as having a waxy or floury texture and there is a scale of 1 – 10 on which varieties are placed. Where potatoes sit on the scale will depend on the amount of dry matter in the potato. For example a floury potato will have a much higher dry matter than a waxy potato.

The potato industry in the UK is the 11th largest producer of the humble spud in the world. The authority that is responsible for regulating, monitoring and promoting this trade is Potato Council. They have several inter linked websites that offer a really fun journey and extremely useful information about literally anything to do with this amazing vegetable. I strongly recommend a visit – especially to the "Love Chips" site. It will certainly complement your decision to read this book. The Council successfully runs National Chip Week every February and works closely with Seafish and the National Federation of Fish Friers and when it comes to the fish and chip industry, there needs to be stability in all these markets for every one to prosper.

My choice for a main crop spud to fry is the mighty Maris Piper. I have tried other – younger - pretenders to the throne but for me, Maris is the champion variety for frying. I usually start with them by the middle of August and stay on them right the way through till June the following year. I choose Maris Piper because it gives me everything I look for in a good frying potato – 10 months availability a year, consistent quality and stable prices, Bold in size, white and fluffy in texture on the inside, golden crispy on the outside and, above all of those things, a flavour that embraces salt and vinegar like a mother does a son returning from war.

I am not alone in this verdict. Maris Piper has been the most popular frying potato for as long as most people can remember but there is a new pretender to the throne emerging and that variety is called Markies. It is a great frying spud that seems to travel well, is more forgiving in that it's robust and doesn't bruise easily. This results in little or no work to do by fish friers before it is ready to chip and fry. I have found it to be a satisfactory alternative but it commands a premium over Maris Piper that I feel is unjustified and does not quite measure up on taste and is frequently a little dry on the palate. It is certainly the variety to look out for and I'm sure it will feature more over the next few years as the tonnages under cultivation increase and the price becomes comparable with other mainstream favourites.

The happy medium

When I move away from variety of spud and talk about what makes the perfect chip, it is important that I embrace as many variables as possible before I give you my preferred winning formula – for if I fail to consider these in my cross examinations then I am sure to fall short of giving a reasonable argument for my conclusions. All we will be left with again is one man's opinion and this will never do in such a far reaching debate.

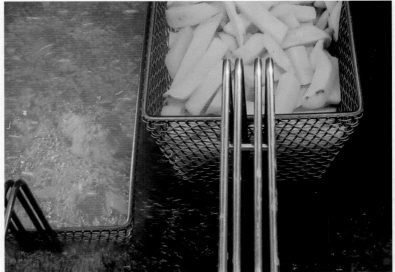

Image courtesy Frying Solutions

Before we explore the makings of the perfect chip, let's explore the frying medium - the choice of which, by the way, goes on and on and on. To make it simple, though, you have basically two types of frying medium – animal or vegetable. From that, there are sub sections all with their own strengths and weaknesses.

Let's deal with vegetable oils first. The types of vegetable oil suitable for frying tend to need additional processing to deliver better stability and life span at high temperatures. Some are blended for taste, others for price and some for colour. In the UK, the most popular veg oil is palm, followed by groundnut (peanut) oil and then rapeseed.

NEODA (the National Edible Oil Distributors Association) regulate and monitor all frying mediums to ensure that they are sourced and processed ethically. There has been much debate about the loss of natural habitat for endangered primates and the "fuel or food" debate but, rest assured, consuming fried food from fish shops can be a guilt free decision. Palm oil makes good bio fuel but is not a viable solution to our motoring headaches. Groundnut oil is being squeezed out by rapeseed oil because of price. Rapeseed imparts less flavour on the product being fried and of course is grown in the UK.

Beef dripping is the preferred frying medium for me because it is natural, traditional, honest and very, very tasty. Beef dripping leaves chips dry, it gives chips a flavour that reminds people of the good old days and a cling to the roof of your mouth for some time after your meal that makes your pennies go further. When used in modern frying ranges, beef dripping offers virtually the same health properties for frying as any veg oil blend – save that some blends like hydrogenated oils have had links to increased risks of cancer. But don't panic, the veg oil has to be pretty darn fooked and in an extremely degraded state – worse than any fish frier would care to use - before it becomes a potential threat. Beef dripping is natural and does not need fixing - like butter and honey, it has stood the test of time and is not broken. I choose a brand that is claimed to come from the cow within four hours of slaughter, refined but not deodorised (impurities taken out but nothing added.)

> *Beef dripping is the preferred frying medium for me because it is natural, traditional, honest and very, very tasty*

My perfect chip also has to be thick. 17mm by 14mm does it for me. French fries are pathetic and really unhealthy. Thicker chips absorb less fat and middle size chips – especially 12mm by 12mm (the most common frozen chip – yuk) or 14mm by 14mm (the most common chip shop chip) just isn't special. A 14mm by 14mm is what you would expect and I always like to exceed my customer's expectations. A 17mm by 14mm chip is a chunky chip, it's pleasing and irresistible to look at and there's more to get into. Anything bigger though and it starts to look intimidating and becomes a £$%&*" to fry - trust me on this!

My perfect chip now has to be golden brown. Not anaemic and not golden, but left just a few moments longer than most operators usually leave them for - to the point where any longer and they may just start to border on being burnt. This means that some of the sugar content in the potato will caramelise and sweeten the taste. It also means that the outside of my perfect chip will be crunchy and crispy like a brand new fifty pound note and the inside will be as fluffy as a summer cloud.

So there you have it – my perfect chip has to be thick, sweet, crunchy on the outside, fluffy and slightly waxy on the inside, fried in beef dripping and with a golden brown appearance. To really please me, I'd like to find lots of little crunchy ones at the bottom of my cone too, soaked in vinegar and some batter scraps in there as well!

Talking of cones, there does seem to be a shift in recent years with the evolution of packaging plus the affordable convenience of boxes instead of paper. This concerns me as a frier who likes to celebrate the history of the dish. I agree that fish and chips deserves survival space when being taken home but eating a cone of chips down the street is as important to me as red public phone boxes on street corners. They are dying out but the modern technology that has taken over hasn't improved things for the end user at all.

Battered and unbowed

It is widely considered by many that have researched the subject that batter was conceived as a disposable vehicle for the protection of fish during the harsh frying process. Just like an eggshell or the hairy skin of

Arthur Parrington demonstrating the art of battering fish at the NFFF Training School

a coconut, the tough exterior was removed to reveal an inner prize that was the real quarry of the hungry recipient. What supports this theory is that in the infancy of our trade, street vendors sold battered fish cold and it was often passed from hand to hand to hand and probably took on an appearance similar to its filthy surroundings. It is probable that it was discarded at the point of consumption and that the fish was all the customer was intended to eat. It couldn't have been long though before someone ate some batter while still warm and a massive light bulb appeared above his head along with the thought "Blimey! That tastes really yummy!"

About ten seconds after that event, the Secret Batter Recipe was invented...

Even I've got a Secret Batter Recipe. Before I reveal mine though and totally blow your mind, gather your thoughts and take yourself back to the best fish and chips you ever tasted and I bet that the batter played as big a part in what made them special as the fish and the spuds.

> *...the unassuming, low profile marriage guidance counsellor to fish and chips that keeps the relationship on track*

Batter is the unassuming, low profile marriage guidance counsellor to fish and chips that keeps the relationship on track. There is of course in this modern world of convenience, a dozen or so brands of just-add-water chip shop batter mix available. Each one is sufficiently different to complement the individual operator's own particular frying medium, equipment and temperature choices along with their cooking style and this goes a long way to create the magic of what makes your favourite shop unique. An operator may add their own ingredient to make their recipe even more special. They may also have inherited the recipe from their teacher. More common additions include lemon or vinegar, lager or bitter to make beer batter and of course sparkling water to make tempura. But for me - although I have a preferred natural mass-produced batter mix that I use sometimes because it performs as well as my own recipe - there really is nothing out there that will do the job better than self raising flour and water.

That's right. My Secret Batter Mix could not be simpler. A plain flour with a raising agent and cold water - nothing else. You see, my version of this iconic dish goes back to its very roots and makes no attempt whatsoever to pretend to be anything other than an honest, affordable meal. When a meal has literally five basic elements – fish, potato, oil, water and flour then you have the moral high ground. Nothing to declare. Flavours that work together and the opportunity to make your public love it simply by them appreciating the unique way you bring those elements together. I know that I must be what makes my fish and chips so irresistible. It is me that turns the water into wine. I am the one that my customers choose to create their favourite meal of the week.

And so when I fry fish and chips for anyone, there are techniques that I employ that set me apart from any other fish frier. Even staff that I have trained to replicate my product in my absence cannot mimic my instinct or reproduce my assessment process. Without a conscious decision, I decide how often I turn fish in the pan, when it has had exactly the perfect amount of time. How I coat every individual piece of fish in batter and how I place it into the hot pan, at what height I let go of the fish and where I put the next one in relation to the previous one are all factors in what makes me and my wares unique. How I manage my frying medium, set the levels and rotate it along with the temperature I choose to fry at only serve to muddy the waters even further.

Given the same five ingredients, it is remarkable just how different other friers' products will be. Removing as many variables as possible can liberate a frier from his daily routine but understand that if you spend too much time away, you will have to accept that even though your customers are getting a reasonable incarnation, they will not be getting the real deal.

And on the side...

Nowadays there are loads of different regional extras to go on the side of your plate. I am not sure when they appeared or what they were called originally but depending on where you may be, there is always

something to go with your fish and chips. Mushy peas must be the best mate to fish and chips. If Fish and Chips were going to kick a ball about in the park, they would stop on the way and ask Mushy Peas if they were coming too.

We like to steep our own peas and boil them on site in total preference to opening a tin and micro-waving ready prepared peas. I dislike very much the way we have become a nation of convenience. We don't seem to repair anything anymore – we simply go out and buy a new one. Things don't seem to be built to last and companies rely on our laziness and poor build quality to sell more products.

With fish and chips though, I refuse to behave in this way. I rely on my quality to bring customers back in and haven't diluted quality or working practices to save money. With mushy peas, there are operators who open a tin that someone else has prepared. This is the first step down a slippery slope – before you know it, they will be buying in frozen chips and so on and so on. Fish and chips is unchanged in 150 years because it isn't broken. We have embraced new technology but good operators stick to traditional methods of production. This gives us a far superior product and healthier margins.

One should never underestimate the potential of really strong mushy pea sales – it's the financial cherry on the cake for a fish frier. Curry sauce is also popular these days but it is nearly always spiced in the safe zone and rarely requires a toilet roll in the fridge. To really please a curry sauce fan, it had better be thick. Gravy, baked beans, bread cakes, barm cakes, baps, tartare sauce sachets, pickled onions, eggs and wallies are all there to make the experience complete. Even I confess to being a bit partial to a mushy pea and brown sauce combo.

Wrapping it up

I firmly believe that fish and chips begins to die the moment it leaves the pan. The very best fish and chips are consumed on site or in the street, straight away. Wrap the meal up and it dies even faster. But if you are not eating it there and then, your meal will need to be transported to its place of consumption. The evolution of fish and chip packaging makes for some interesting reading.

The fried fish and chip trade must be one of the first industries to properly recycle other peoples unwanted goods - long before tree huggers made it trendy. Our industry wrapped its core product up in newspaper and many argue that it never tasted as good again after that came to an end in the early eighties. In the early days, the only way working class folk even got to know what was happening in the news was by buying fish and chips. There were some pretty serious hygiene issues relating to the ink used, which contained lead, and was also made from old motor oil which was considered unsafe and outlawed. The paper itself though was a good insulator and soaked up excess grease and vinegar and still remains popular today without any print on it at all. Nowadays, newspaper ink is again safe but packaging and customers' expectations have evolved too. Cardboard, polystyrene and even newer bio-degradable boxes have taken over. They have the same insulating properties but offer fish and chips survival space which means they are presented better at the end of their journey. They are also easier to eat out of when on the go but don't let me persuade you if you are a diehard white paper fan. I'm just happy that you've found something that works for you.

One weakness of fish and chips is that it doesn't travel very well. It's perfect finger food and great to eat "on the go" but sweats, goes soggy and clumps together when steam is not allowed to vent and it becomes squashed into confined spaces. Our great-grannies probably had the best idea, when they would take their own beautifully decorated china bowls to the fish and chip shop to collect their family's supper, and then walk it home covered loosely with a clean cloth. We are getting better though at finding more modern solutions and packaging nowadays is designed to create survival space for the meal, keep the heat in and allow the steam to escape (that's why there are little gaps in the side of the boxes and holes drilled out).

Is the price right?

The price of fish and chips is another hot topic for debate and it has been known for me to get quite animated about this subject. There are several reasons why I see red mist on this matter – especially when people start to argue that fish and chips are becoming too expensive.

The real problem starts with the fact that fish and chips is most commonly sold in the High Street. There are now so many rubbish meals for sale in the High Street that fish and chips get bundled into the same group as them by mistake. How many ways can man invent a mangled, cheaper cut of processed meat with loads of bulking agents and flavourings and slap it between one or two slices of carbohydrate? Burgers, Hotdogs, Baguettes, Naan rolls, Chapattis, Tortillas, Paninis, Sandwiches, Subs, Kebabs etc etc. Do I need to go on? Then of course we have national dishes too like pizza, curry, stir fry and tapas. When you compare all – yes all - of these other meals, how many are made from raw materials that are claimed straight from nature and not messed about with in any way? How many of those other meals cost more in time, effort and expense to produce? Consider the journey from sea to plate that a piece of fish makes – the skilled hands required and the delicacy of the raw material. It is handled with respect, skill and care rather than twisted and added to and stretched to make go further. It still resembles its natural state when it arrives on your plate.

I would like you to consider now the running costs of a fish and chip shop. Try to relate that back to the unit cost of a portion of chips. At my site in Ely for example, a portion of chips in my restaurant - served on a plate with a knife and fork costs £1.80 and includes salt and vinegar. That is a mere 30 pence more than it costs to take a portion of chips away. I have to extract from the price I set for a portion of chips whether a customer is to eat in or sit down, all raw material costs (spuds, beef dripping, paper, salt and vinegar) labour costs (peeling the spuds, frying the chips, serving the chips, clearing the tables, washing the dishes and cleaning the shop) and running costs (rent, gas, electric, water, rates, VAT, capital purchases, repairs and tax on any profit). My rent at Ely is £40,000 per annum, I use £10,000 of beef dripping a year. My labour cost for the year is £80,000. Gas and electric are £8,000 a year. If we do the sum of how much a sack of spuds costs and how many portions we get from a sack, it looks like we are making a killing. I would encourage a customer to do a different calculation and see how many portions of chips you have to sell just to pay the rent!

When the public get brain washed into paying a tenner for a pizza which is essentially cheese on toast, let me tell you I can make literally hundreds of dough balls from one sack of strong flour with olive oil, yeast, salt, sugar and water. Each 12 inch pizza base would cost me about 9 pence to produce.

How much chicken goes into a foil tray of chicken madras? One breast fillet if you're lucky? Consider now, was that chicken selected because it was free range, corn fed and likely to have a better flavour?

Of course not- It was not even bred in the UK and yet once its taste is completely masked in an oily sauce of tinned tomato, curry powder, onions and spices you will stump up seven quid for that and another three bucks for some fluffy boiled rice to go with it. I can source burgers for 14 pence each and buns for 12 pence each. Imagine how cheap they are when you are McDonalds.

> *The closer you look at rivals the more you see just what a fantastic and honest meal fish and chips really is*

Their pound saver menu has less nutritional value than a house brick and is priced for them to more than break even believe me. The closer you look at rivals the more you see just what a fantastic and honest a meal fish and chips really is. It really doesn't belong in the High Street any longer.

It should have earned its place decades ago onto the menus in all the top restaurants like lobster has or the best parts of a cow. Yet it remains in with the riff raff not because it is still so cheap to produce but because we have evolved as an industry to mass-produce it for less than we should in order to attract enough customers to meet the rising costs required for us to remain in business.

Fish and chips should be at least double its price if it had only risen in line with inflation over the last 30 years. I have trained chefs to fry haddock and chips in one of London's top eateries and customers there pay £46.50 for essentially the same dish as all of my fellow high street chippies sell. The only difference is the environment in which it is sold and perhaps the customers' bank balances. Rich people aren't stupid or careless with money - haddock and chips is by far the most popular choice on the menu at this fine dining establishment and the chefs called me in to teach them how to re-create the dish as close to authentic chip shop style as possible.

At less than a fiver, many shops are in serious danger of pricing themselves into oblivion as rising costs and increased competition are making it harder than ever to make a profit without high volumes of sales. My message is simple then… Realise the value of your fish supper and accept that it deserves to be more than most other takeaways in the high street even though right now it is probably the cheapest.

So there you have the basic elements to the dish itself – honest raw materials, handled by skilled tradesmen all along the supply chain from field or ocean to plate, created passionately and served with pride, usually for under a fiver. But where did it all begin?

Chapter Two – the history lesson

Every family has a poor relative that is never spoken about. Whether they're still very much alive or in the distant memory of a passing generation there's no denying the awkward and uncomfortable path many of us choose to tread when trying to prevent our "social veneer" from coming away and exposing what we should be able to embrace as history or heritage. I'm not sure if with every new generation, we strive to improve our social standing or that some of us give way to peer pressure and prefer to hide our humble beginnings. I for one am proud that my grandfather was a bin-man (or should I say refuse contractor?) and the other owned a sweet shop (I mean confectionery retail outlet!)

Earliest origins

The marriage between battered fish and chipped potato is not a Cinderella story. Both independent trades were of questionable lineage and even in their best light can only be considered bastard sons and daughters of less than glamorous professions. Before they even met and fell in love, both battered fish and chipped potato each have an interesting past that is worth exploring individually for their humble, diverse and often quite unpleasant journey to their serendipitous date with destiny.

The fried chip and battered fish trade should never have prevailed. So squalid and unsanitary were the early days of it all that even the poorest classes despised anyone who undertook to practice their profession in their neighbourhood. Without regulation, the smell from the cooking and the storage of the raw materials was horrendous. The raw materials were of the poorest quality, the frying techniques extremely primitive and the finished product distributed from hand to hand by street sellers once cooled. "Dabs", as already mentioned, were the cheapest and most available flat fish at the time that the fried fish trade emerged. Whoever started the London scene had probably been introduced to the fried fish idea thanks to the Jewish refugees from Portugal and Spain who brought the dish to England in the 18th Century. Charles Dickens can claim the first mention of a fried fish warehouse in Oliver Twist, which was first published in 1838.

I will resist for now for drawing my line in the sand and committing to when fish first met chips or vice versa. My research has revealed several accounts that demonstrate that there was a very real dislike for the whole fried fish trade that emerged in London. The "dabs" were usually plaice or sole and were surplus or left over stock that a fishmonger didn't manage to sell, or stock that had become tired and was no longer good enough to sell. Rather than make a total loss, the fishmonger would dispose of this stock at a discount. The purchaser would take this whole fish to his place of business, wash it if he were conscientious, remove the head, fins and guts and dip it in a flour and water mix before frying it in dark oil.

The best way to describe the frying equipment is in a similar vein to that of primitive clothes washing boiler apparatus. It was simply a metal dome shaped bowl filled with oil, sat on top of a three walled brick construction with one open space making what would be the fourth wall of a square. This opening allowed a coal fire to be built and maintained underneath the bowl. When the fire was too high the oil might be too hot and the "dabs" be ruined and when the fire became too low, the fish might not cook properly at all. It is safe to say that consistency was virtually impossible to achieve. The aromas of old smoke, oil and short dated fish filled the air, seeped into the fabric of the building and caused a nuisance to neighbouring properties and streets. Many landlords at this time refused to grant permission for this kind of activity on the grounds that it rendered a property unfit for any other occupation once a fried fish operation had been undertaken.

> *The aromas of old smoke, oil and short dated fish filled the air...*

At this point in history, your average fish frier usually came from the community he grew up in. He would be poorly educated but might well know his regular customers by name. It would be highly likely that he would be completely ignorant of any obligations with regard to health and safety, hygiene or laws of sanitation. The Medical Officer of Health for London County Council in 1906 was Sir Shirley Murphy, who retrospectively recalls several details about the early fried fish trade, including a comment that in the exhibition year of 1851 there were a few fried fish shops. By 1861 there were at least 300 individuals documented as operating fried fish businesses in London. Without any regulation, the product would be sold in the streets and not from the site where it was cooked. Dirty hands would "fumble" through the seller's wares to find a piece they liked the look of. It goes without saying that being at the front of the queue was always preferred. Sir Shirley also recalls that as far back as 1856 fried fish was occasionally sold with baked potatoes but that by 1871 their place had been taken by chipped potatoes "a la mode", introduced - according to him - from France.

The Belgians just down the road, however, have records of "husky chips of potatoes fried with some reluctant drops of oil" - Charles Dickens again, in A Tale of Two Cities - as far back as 1781 and the tradition of frying potatoes carved into various shapes, including fish, dates back further still to at least 1680.

Whilst the London scene of fried dabs emerged, up in Oldham there was an increasing supply and growing demand for deep fried chipped potatoes. The very first "chip shop" is widely accepted as being on the site of Tommyfield Market in Oldham itself, and range manufacturer Henry Nuttall have always claimed to have built a frying range in 1865 for this establishment, run by a Mr Dyson.

The where, the who and the when

As to when and where fish and chips came together, this is where the smelly brown stuff really hits the fan….

In Mossley, Lancashire, a Mr John Lees is credited by his descendants with pioneering the concept of battered fish with chipped potatoes in 1863. In that year, he and his wife were running a small wooden hut on the market selling pea soup and pig's trotters when he returned from a trip to Oldham with the idea of "Chipped potatoes in the French and American style", and put a sign up over his hut to that effect. When the huts were pulled down in the 1890s, the Lees moved to a permanent erection on the other side of the street where a new sign in the window said "Chip Potato Restaurant - oldest established in the world" - later changed to read "The oldest fish and chip shop in the world."

Conflicting accounts, again from family members, state that Joseph Malin opened the first combined fish and chip shop in Cleveland Street in London in 1860, and as late as the 1970s, Malin's carried a sign over their shops which said "Estd 1860". It was to this family that the National Federation of Fish Friers, after much debate and research, awarded a 100-year plaque in 1963.

So there has been a North/South divide consisting of claim and counter claim as to who owns the right to be credited as the match maker in the greatest culinary double act of all time. I must freely admit that I have relied upon the fantastic in-depth research carried out by Wendy Durham - editor of Fish & Chips and Fast Food Magazine - an experienced historical researcher who has delved deeper than anyone before her into government records and census archives, as well as personal family accounts, in her quest to unearth some hard evidence to support either the north or the south claims. During her expedition, Wendy came across an even more amazing story in a third claim regarding a woman whose shops were based in middle England - Yorkshire to be exact - and was known affectionately as Granny Duce. Clara "Granny" Duce was a remarkable woman who opened a chain of shops and had almost a football team of kids in a time before women were even allowed to vote. What makes her story even more special is that even to this day - five generations later - there is still an unbroken chain of Duces running fish and chip shops in the South of England. Her claim to the throne deserves to be aknowledged as being just as significant as the Lees and Malin claims.

You see, Wendy discovered that there was no documentary evidence to support the presence of fried fish at the Lees shop until after the 1901 census and when double checking the research, she discovered that the Malins did not admit to being fish and chip folk before the 1891 census. However, doing fish and chips was not a highly regarded occupation at that time, and many might not have wanted to officially admit to it. In fact, Henry Mayhew, writing in "London Labour and the London Poor" in 1861, states that of the 300 or so fish friers in London at that time, hardly any bothered to complete census forms, and even fewer stated their correct occupation. It's also important to remember that in those days, census enumerators were considered to be in league with the tax collectors, and viewed with suspicion - so any lucrative business conducted by the wife and/or kids "on the side" would have been concealed, usually without fear of discovery, as the enumerator was interested only in the occupation of the household "head". This concealment was aided by the nature of the business, which involved selling the product on the street and not from the premises where it was produced.

An enumerator calls...
Photo courtesy National Archives and Records Administration

Which possibly explains why the Malins steadfastly give their occupation in the census as hearthrug weavers - every single blooming one of them, except one who is a bootmaker. In 1891 Joseph Henry Malin at last admits to being a fishmonger in Cleveland Street, and has his two daughters working as a potato peeler and a fish frier - pretty conclusive stuff, but 30 years too late. John William Malin also seems to have started before that year at Old Ford Road, and by

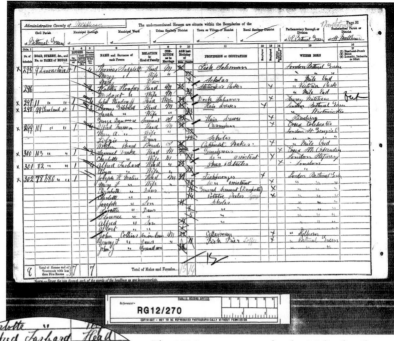

The 1891 census entry for the Malin family
Image courtesy of the National Archives

1901 his son John Charles Malin had moved out into Goldsmiths Row with his first shop. Wendy made contact with one of the present-day family who has also failed to find links to fish and chips earlier than 1891.

The Cleveland street property did not become a fish and chip shop officially until sometime between 1881 and 1891, having been listed as a carpenter's shop and a dairy - amongst others - in earlier years. It does not appear in the 1880 Post Office Directory, either, although by that year there are many fried fish shops and fried fish dealers listed in the new "Fried Fish Dealers" section of the Directory. That said, it was more than likely that for almost twenty odd years the Malins went about their business without declaring it.

It was no different with John and Martha Lees and their family, who were officially cotton workers in Saddleworth until 1891, when we find John Lees listed as a Refreshment Room Keeper in the 1891 Mossley census. They didn't admit to being in the frying trade until 1901 when

118 Lumb Lane, Bradford, today - the site of one of Clara Duce's 1891 fish and chip shops

the "Chip Potato Restaurant" was listed under the management of Channing Lees - one of John's sons - with Martha Lees in residence at the same address.

Yet in spite of the lack of evidence, family sources place both these families as pioneering fish and chips early in the 1860s.

The Duces also don't emerge as fish friers until the 1890s, when the street directories and census entries show that at least three fried fish shops - as well as a grocer's - were being operated in Bradford by various members of the family. However the legend of Clara Duce as a Yorkshire lass doesn't stand up to scrutiny - she was born in 1845 in Bushey, Hertfordshire and by 1901 had returned there with her family to start a Southern fish and chip empire, parts of which survive to this day. You could say that whilst the Lees and the Malins represent a North/South divide, Clara brings both North and South to our tale!

So that's the story so far - plenty of anecdote, lots of family memories, but no hard documentary evidence of fish and chips being cooked together by any of our "founding families" before 1891.

I have reasoned and argued with another far more deserving and thorough investigator into the origins of fish and chips about committing to a concrete theory. But both Kelvin Baines – a passionate champion of our trade - and Wendy Durham have exhausted all lines of enquiry in their quest for answers. It's not because I was born and bred in Lewisham nor is it that I have any prejudices against northern folk (in fact I am definitely of the opinion that proper fish and chips must be cooked in beef dripping – a practice much aligned with northern techniques!) that I am for the purposes of promotion, probability and plain old propaganda going to plant my flag and go with the most widely accepted theory that the birth place of fish and chips may have been as early as 1860 and is likely to have been in London.

This will upset many folk. It will upset them even more when I confess that the main reasons I have committed to this theory are that London was the most concentrated growth area for fish and chip shops in the years between 1851 and the turn of the century, and as an industry, we need to firmly cement a time and place that we can anchor celebrations to in years to come. In 2010, for example, our nation's favourite dish is 150 years old. This is big news indeed and should be celebrated with whole streets partying and day trips to the coast and Union Jacks waving! The most British thing in the world, born in the UK from French, Spanish, Portuguese and Belgian ancestors, deserves recognition for such a unique achievement.

Without a time machine we will never know for certain whether the first fish and chips were fried together by a Malin, a Lees or a Duce, or perhaps by an as yet undiscovered pioneer, and we will never be sure whether it was in the North or South – but we can say this....1860 in London is a pretty darn good guess.

The early years

From the humblest of beginnings - and it doesn't really matter where - there came this marriage. It was forged in the coals which were driving an emerging industrial superpower - an affordable meal for everyone that was easy to consume, portable and delicious. I compare the growth of fish and chips as a trade in those days to the appearance of the Internet in recent times. Before, there was nothing quite like it and it changed things forever.

In the 50 years that followed its birth, the numbers of fish and chip retailers grew at an incredible rate with little or no change in the development of techniques or basic principles of operation. The equipment was still so primitive that by 1910 the Ministry of Health had decided it was time to impose some basic compliances to improve the environment that greeted the buying public who frequented these establishments – in particular a glass screen enclosure around all commercial frying ranges, as they had become to be known.

It has been suggested that Battersea in London is so named because of the high concentration of fish and chip shops and the manner in which the pans would spit and throw oil and batter indiscriminately about the walls, ceilings and floors therein. At this time, there was still no solution to the smoke, steam and smell that resulted from the manufacturing process and the conclusion was what can only be described as an undesirable miasma that found its way out of the building and often into and onto neighbouring properties, creating a very real nuisance.

The French and the Americans had already tried to launch their own respective fish and chip industries. They failed miserably to succeed on both counts, partly because fish and chips was mass-produced in really

Steam trawler Dias/Viola, built in 1906 at Beverley in East Yorkshire for the Hellyer Steam Fishing Company of Hull

appalling conditions for the operator. But the industrial revolution had advanced the Englishman's thirst for development and by now the nation already had such a strong dependence on fish and chips that it was not too long before huge steps were being made, by manufacturers and entrepreneurs alike, who recognised both the need and the demand for a more professional, reliable and practical operation for the now serious operator.

Whilst the French and the Americans gave up, the Brits were already making significant advances in both hygiene practices and community standing.

The trade matures...

The Public Health Act of 1875 and localised county councils brought guidelines and a basic framework of good practice to the trade, paying particular attention to the materials used for frying, the removal of smoke from shops, the preparation techniques for fish and suitability of premises for the purpose of operating a fried fish and chip shop.

Bespoke equipment had been designed and constructed to assist the operator in the preparation of potatoes for frying. These machines could both remove the dirt and skin from a potato and cut them into chips. The old brick built frying apparatus had been replaced by purpose built coal-fired frying ranges constructed of non-porous materials and with canopies or flues for extracting the smoke, steam and oil vapours from the building and into the open air outside. This made conditions much cleaner inside and also communicated to the local residents with its distinctive aroma that the shop was frying up and ready for business.

This is the point in fish and chips history that our romantic attachments begin. Everyone has a memory of the almost magnetic allure of that familiar smell that literally pulled its patrons in without prejudice or remorse and now it had become a part of every day life.

At this time the daily catch would come from vessels that did exactly that – go out and come back in daily. The industrial revolution saw the emergence of steam-powered boats that could stay out longer. The Brits had a fairly good relationship with Iceland who would allow them to use their ports for shelter in stormy weathers as long as they kept their nets and fishing gear stowed. In return we agreed not to fish within a boundary set by two extreme land points that are far too Icelandic for me to type or for you to try and read. In the years that followed, the Icelandic government tried to protect its country's main source of industry, employment and revenue by extending the zones in which foreign vessels were not allowed to catch fish. The British government did not recognise this and so the Cod Wars arose as a result.

...and gathers momentum

Being a Master Frier was now as respected a trade as a butcher, baker or candlestick maker - unless of course you were not very good at it! By 1910 in London alone there were in excess of 1,200 fish and chip shops.

By 1913 the National Federation of Fish Friers had been born out of a lesser-known association started in Lancaster in 1907. Now with a voice and representation at the highest level, the fish and chip industry was unstoppable. As frying equipment advanced in its sophistication and with many communities benefiting from a gas supply, the first really significant step in the evolution of fish and chip shops came with the production of more efficient gas-powered bespoke frying ranges. They were slow to take off in their early conception, not due to the cost of acquiring such a cutting edge piece of equipment, but because of their running costs versus the conventional coal or coke fired pans, which, at this time, were almost half the price to run.

The busiest shops recognised the benefits of gas - a more consistent product could be turned out in greater volumes due to the controllability of the gas burners and it was much cleaner to work with and was setting apart this type of establishment from its lesser rivals. Fish and Chip Emporiums were beginning to move out of the back alleys and into the high streets. Now firmly cemented into the British way of life, the weekly or sometimes daily pilgrimage to the local chippy was now an affordable treat for most families – often with a fight over who would get to go and fetch them. Any fish frier worth his salt knew most of his customers by

name and almost always "performed" in his shop to his customers like a master of ceremonies would to his guests – maintaining a friendly rapport at all times and setting a tone that made waiting for the meal almost as pleasurable as the dish itself.

The most famous frier in our past has to be Harry Ramsden whose first shop was in Guisley West Yorkshire. It was started in 1928 in a wooden hut in White Cross in close proximity to a bus terminal and within three years had moved to what has been described by many as a fish and chip "palace." Rumoured to have styled his palace on the Ritz, with wooden panelling, carpets and chandeliers, Harry Ramsden was a true marketeer who was simply years ahead of his time.

Harry realized that he could spread the word about his product with the use of merchandising and offered diners a unique opportunity at the time to eat affordable food in a luxurious environment. Customers always left with a memento or souvenir from their visit and the word soon spread.

Harry Ramsden was the first operator to introduce thermostats to the trade in his shop in Guisley and insisted that they showed 350 degrees F before his friers started to cook anything. God help anyone who didn't follow this basic rule imposed by the boss!

War service

Even today large multiples and giant fast food chains cannot re-create the experience that one gets from frequenting the local fish shop, and its place in the heart of the nation was carved out forever during the Second World War, when Britain's 35,000 fish and chip shops played a pivotal role in securing victory over the Germans. The Territorial Army used specially adapted tents to provide fish and chips to soldiers before battles and the Minister for Food - Francis Lord Woolton - deemed fish and chips to be such an important meal that he refused to ration it. The three raw materials required to produce it were the same three raw materials that the Germans could not deny us. Being an island virtually surrounded by the enemy, we were still able to catch fish, grow potatoes and mine coal.

The British Rail network - as we came to know it - was configured during the Second World War to ensure that these three commodities could be easily transported to all four corners of the country to keep the nation from starving. At this time there was a fish and chip shop for every 900 people in England – many of them, rumoured to be up to a third at its highest point, were mobile and serviced small villages and rural communities. Word soon got around when a frier had a delivery of fish and people often queued for hours to get a meal. There are even stories of some shops employing doormen to control crowds.

Fish would often be collected from the local railway station by the chippy owner, freshly delivered from the docks – Grimsby on the East coast being the main distribution centre at this time. It would arrive in large containers packed in cracked ice ready for the frier to skin, bone and cut into portions before frying for the hungry masses.

Britain's 35,000 fish and chip shops played a pivotal role in securing victory over the Germans

Potatoes on the other hand were sourced locally and were generally of Maris Piper or King Edward variety. The spuds were then rumbled by machine or in some cases peeled by hand, cleaned up to remove any blemishes and finally chipped into baths of water before being drained and cooked in batches for queues of customers often carrying their own containers or dishes. Even at this time some ranges were still coal-fired and the quality of the product depended on the skill of the frier. There was no reason why a shop from this period should smell offensive anymore. Refrigeration was widely available and ranges had sumps and fans and filters. According to one theory at the time, smells are carried in moisture, so that by passing the exhaust over cold metal plates, the moisture could be condensed and only dry air, free of odour, would be discharged.

The golden years

After the war, the Fifties and the Sixties were a golden era for the fish and chip supper. The first Cod War with Iceland occurred in 1958 when the no-fishing zone for foreign vessels was introduced by the Icelandic government, which took the original boundary from 4 nautical miles to 12. Things became so heated at that time that the British Navy had to escort our fishing boats to protect them.

With very little in the high street to class as competition, a strong network of independent retailers became well established, although

frying fish and chips still remained a very highly skilled job. Preparing the raw materials, managing the frying medium and the execution of frying itself with pans that fluctuated in temperature greatly made it almost an art form and many customers would insist on having their meal cooked by the regular chap and no one else. It was not until many years later, with the introduction of more modern frying equipment, that we began to see chains of shops under the same name start to appear, because it was virtually impossible to keep the quality up at the shops where you were not working.

It was almost a sin at the time, too, if a skilled and well patronised fish frier were to prosper and afford himself a new home or car and elevate his social standing above that of his customers. It was quite common and well documented for friers at the time to hide the fact that they might be doing well for themselves. I well recall that my father bought his first Mercedes in 1983 and remember even more clearly how he suffered at the hands of his spending audience one Saturday morning when the word had spread!

This period saw fish and chips enjoy the most stable time in its history. Décor moved with the times and legislation kept the trade up to date and even though the number of outlets reduced as the country recovered from its participation in the two world wars, fish and chips was already firmly established as a keystone in a very British way of life.

Changing times and lifestyles

Now, as the world seemed to get smaller and smaller, new threats to the trade started to appear on the horizon, along with innovations that had the potential to revolutionise the fish and chip trade yet again.

As the years rolled by, the family unit started to change. Every generation strove for even higher standards of living and, to enable this, the role of women in the household evolved at the same time. Equal rights for women is another book by another author and being a modern man, I fully support this progress and appreciate that there is still some way to go. The family dynamic is quite relevant at this particular time in the evolution of fish and chips as more women began to carve out careers and work full time. They did this as well as being full time mums and housewives. This brought more disposable income into the household but at the same time added pressure to the family's ability to eat a home cooked meal every day. Many women

still managed what most men – if they are honest - couldn't and that was to juggle the domestic demands as well as any new professional obligations. This lifestyle change was good for fish and chips. It still represented affordable, nutritious and convenient food for the masses and was still considered a treat - even if consumed several times a week - and it became a popular meal solution for everyone when both parents were working.

Fish and chips became multi-cultural from the 1960's onwards, embracing new nationalities and diversifying. In England, Scotland, Ireland and Wales, an influx of migrants entered the business and picked up the basics of the trade on their travels. The Italians arrived first, and found it to be an open trade into which they could readily move. The first of these families came from just six villages in Tuscany and to this day they still return to their homeland to participate in a festival called the "Feast of the Mules" when they prepare fish and chips for the local inhabitants. Cypriots and Chinese also entered the trade in vast numbers at this time, my father being one of them. Its accessible and family- orientated structure opened up opportunities for working men to move into self-employment, working alongside their wives and children. One should not forget the importance of the trade in opening up opportunities for all nationalities to contribute in their own unique ways to the nation's greatest dish. This legacy is continued today by the offspring of those early migrants who came to our shores in search of a better life for their families and found it in fish and chips. Many shops changed hands, with many British born friers exiting the trade, and with that a new multi-cultural chapter began. This new generation of friers had new challenges to face and less money than the previous generation with which to progress their businesses.

Competition in the High Street

Other take away meals were now starting to emerge and as it became easier and more affordable to move from country to country, there came a huge wave of new food offers to the high street that represented real competition for fish and chips for the first time in its hundred year history.

Back in 1930 on the other side of the Atlantic, at the dining table in the private quarters of a service station in Corbin, Kentucky, a Colonel Sanders had used his $105.00 social security cheque to start serving his own brand of fried chicken to hungry travellers. In 1965 the Colonel's secret recipe Kentucky Fried Chicken first appeared on our shores – in Preston to be precise - and KFC became the first US fast food quick service restaurant to enter the UK.

Meanwhile in America in 1954, Ray Kroc had become the first official appointed franchisee of a burger chain formed in 1940 by two brothers, Dick and Mac McDonald. Twenty years later in 1974 in Woolwich, South East London, the 3,000th worldwide and first-ever McDonalds site opened in the UK, Wimpy having already arrived some years earlier.

On paper, all these food offers were no match for fish and chips. It was junk food in its purest form and was not initially received at all well by us Brits. However, they had arrived at a time when the fish and chip industry was very exposed. Two more Cod Wars took place in 1972 and 1975 with Iceland increasing its no fishing zone to protect its own industry and preserve its cod stocks from over fishing – first from 12 to 50 nautical miles and then from 50 to 200 nautical miles. This news instilled a conscience and a lot of misinformation into the British public, who were led to believe that the ocean had been over-fished and that the fish and chip industry was to blame.

The Americans had got their act together and knew exactly where the weaknesses were in fish and chips' armour. As a network of independent retailers, the fish and chip industry consisted of thousands of individual small business entrepreneurs, save for one or two small chains. These friers had always relied on local reputation and word of mouth to promote their businesses and were oblivious in many cases to the benefits or advantages of marketing and advertising. If any activity of this kind was undertaken, it was to promote their own name or brand and not that of fish and chips.

Even today, the brand and image of our nation's favourite meal is firmly rooted in the past because the industry has never united as a common marketing force to deliver all the positive messages about the umbrella brand of fish and chips. All independent shops get to trade and use the brand name of fish and chips for free and spend all their marketing budgets promoting their own name..

Uncle Sam invaded quickly and without remorse...

Uncle Sam invaded quickly and without remorse. In 1976 McDonalds hit the UK TV screens with their first advert. Their branding was slick, their restaurants all looked the same and they made a visit to their restaurants appear glamorous. They had introduced a clown character called Ronald in 1963 who – like the Pied Piper of Hamelyn – almost whisked away a whole generation of kids from fish and chips to their burgers, fries and thick shakes. With an absolutely massive marketing budget and the ability to write cheques as big as necessary to secure prominent locations, they grew at an incredible rate. The key to their success was down to one basic element across their whole operation. Consistency.

Consistency was never going to be a strength for thousands of independent fish and chip shops all with different oils, batters and portion sizes.

Our strength had always been in the product itself and the relationships that shop owners forged with their community of customers. The Americans gave consumers consistent products, consistent service and food that was even easier to eat than fish and chips. It didn't matter that it had far less nutritional value as no one was questioning it at the time anyway.

Fish and chips was powerless to fight back. Not even the NFFF (National Federation of Fish Friers) could persuade all the independent retailers to put their hands in their pockets to buy advertising and compete with the big chains' marketing machines and - even today - the image of our National Treasure remains firmly cemented in the past because of this.

As more ethnic outlets started to appear with exotic, spicy and rice dishes, they took a further chunk of the takeaway food market, focusing on trade later in the evening. During the mid eighties, as standards of living grew and the service industry exploded, the fish and chip market stayed level at best and declined in most cases. Fish friers were afraid to protect their profit margins for fear of losing business and kept their prices low, even though costs to them were going up. Empowered women were at this time being bombarded with messages about health and fitness as well as being almost smothered by images of unrealistic female perfection. This was huge business and fish and chips was an easy target – often being depicted as unhealthy because it was deep fried. As an industry we responded by saying very little. The American chains went legal on anyone who dared suggest their food was bad and so fish and chips bore the brunt of the storm even though it was actually healthier food than other high street rivals.

A technological fix

In about 1985 the fish and chip industry in the UK was injected with a new strain of frying technology by an unlikely hero who was a fish frier himself and, by pure coincidence, was just 15 miles from where I was starting out on my first serious attempt at being a Master Frier. His name was Chris Boyle and he revolutionised what had been one of the most rigid and basic principles of frying fish and chips in the UK.

It came about from a trip to Holland. Like most innovators, though, his work ended up being the catalyst for someone else's success. Boyle is rightly credited with bringing the concept to the UK, but it could never have revolutionised the industry under his control because Chris didn't have the ability to convince the whole frying community that what he had discovered was special. I want to go into detail about what he was doing and so I need to explain the earlier principle of frying first and then explain what Boyle had discovered in Holland and how he first brought this innovative technology to the UK.

Traditional frying equipment typically had any number of pans and they were usually all the same – square and deep. During the process of frying, some oil or dripping would be absorbed into the fish and chips and when levels became low, they would be topped up with fresh or if they were dark, sometimes removed. This job was laborious and messy – not only that, but in order to keep the oil or dripping in the

*A modern
HE Dutch range from
Hewigo, the pioneers in the UK*

best condition, friers had discovered years before that the best way was to cook fish in the pan followed by chips, followed by fish and then followed by chips and so on. The chips would take some of the batter bits with them and clean the frying medium.

But the Dutch - driven by government-led power-saving incentives - had developed a new method of frying that meant that fish was fried in shallow square pans and chips were fried in deeper round pans. The Dutch had discovered that round pans cooked chips faster and more evenly and as well as that, they had designed and fitted built-in filtration systems to all the pans which made cleaning the frying medium almost effortless. At the push of a button, oil or dripping could be removed, cleaned and put back into any pan and this in itself would save a frier literally hours of work each week and improve the taste of his product and the longevity of his frying medium. Not only that, but friers would find it far easier than before to achieve consistency in their product - which had proven to be one of the keys to the huge success of big chain operators like McDonalds.

Made by Hewigo, the Dutch ranges were imported by Boyle, who

*Chef Brian Turner
trying out the
Florigo Dutch range
at Petrou Brothers
in Chatteris*

changed the name on them when they arrived in the UK to Planet and marketed them in the UK. The new technology was nothing short of absolute bloody genius.

In 1988 Harry Ramsden's, a convert to Dutch ranges, was floated on the London Stock Exchange and was almost stand-alone as the only fish and chip shop chain recognised as a "household" name. In the very same year, the Seafish Industry Authority launched the Official UK Fish and Chip Shop of The Year Competition. In its 22 years to date, more than two thirds of the winners have used Dutch frying ranges, which is quite telling when you consider how few Dutch ranges there still are in the UK. Towards the end of the nineties, Harry Ramsden's was bought by the Granada food service company for £20 million - although it never achieved the ultimate accolade of being crowned the UK number one fish and chip shop.

The Dutch meanwhile had done it again. This time they produced a frying range that not only galvanised the trade, but took the evolution of fish and chips to a new pinnacle, giving it a re-birth as one of the healthiest takeaway meals on the high street today. The principle was simple, the technology was robust and the results were incredible.

> *The new thechnology was nothing short of absolute bloody genius*

In simple terms what the Dutch were able to do was produce a high efficiency (HE) pan that virtually eradicated the drop in oil temperature when raw chips and fish were placed in it. The implications of this monumental leap forward were enormous. It meant that fat absorption, which occurs at low temperatures during the recovery to frying levels, fell dramatically, making fish and chips healthier than most rival take away meals by as much as 40%. It also meant that without the temperature swing, cooking times were even easier to pin-point, making it simple to achieve high and consistent fish and chip quality - every time - without the skill factor.

The ability to train any competent frier to operate one of these new ranges was the final piece of the puzzle that allowed operators to "roll out" their brand and open multi-site chains. The most professional operators were now able to do exactly that. One particularly worthy of a mention is Hugh Lipscombe and his Fish 'n' Chick'n chain of shops. Although he does not feature in my "Five of the Best" chapter, Hugh has to be recognised for being the largest single independent chain in modern times. Born into a fish frying family and very passionate about the trade, Hugh is also a very smart businessman who is organised, professional and accomplished. He epitomises the latest generation of fish and chip operators but in his own unassuming and very measured

Latest Dutch range technology from KFE-Kiremko

kind of way. I would describe his brand as safe, uncomplicated and reliable – just like his menu, shops and service.

Hugh doesn't cut corners when it comes to quality and practices and sticks closely to the principles under which fish and chips sells the best – as a consistent, affordable, reliable meal. Any one of his shops is capable of winning awards and does so frequently.

Another chain with a brand very worthy of a mention as this chapter finishes is George's Tradition based in the Midlands - the winner of Best Multiple Retailer at the 2009/10 chip shop awards ceremony.

2000 and beyond

As we reached the Millennium, the number of fish and chips shops was stable at around 10,000 in the UK. There was a clear divide starting to appear between those shops that had kept up with the times and invested in new equipment that enabled them to evolve and those shops that were somewhat time-warped but nevertheless still persevering and surviving.

Fish and chips still hadn't broken through the five pound barrier per portion, mainly due to the continued fear from owners that their trade levels would suffer if they raised their prices. By now 95% of all shops were sourcing their cod responsibly from sustainable stocks where measures are in place to prevent over fishing. The scare stories in the papers and on the news only relate to North Sea stocks which represent just 4-5% of the global cod market and are rarely seen in fish and chip shops.

As I come to the closing words of this history lesson, the end of the first decade in the new millennium is upon us and fish and chips has reached its 150th birthday. The industry finds itself in a High Street full of diversity and competition, where the best operators are setting higher standards than most big fast food chains, with a level of service that is unrivalled.

The product itself has never been better for you due to the HE pan technology, and when compared to most other takeaways, fish and chips still wins hands down on value for money, costing less today in relation to an average week's wages than it did ten, twenty or even thirty years ago. It has a lower fat content than its rivals, there is plenty more (sustainable) fish in the sea and the nation's favourite dish is still produced with no colourings, additives, flavourings, enhancers or any other hidden nasties (that is especially true if you come to my shop!)

The product is better than ever and so is the value. The challenge faced by the fish and chip industry today is finding a way to unite and re-educate the nation – not the existing customers - but the ones that got away...

Chapter Three - one man's story of a lifetime in the frying trade

If you think after reading this chapter that it is a little self indulgent, then you are right. This is my book (well technically it's yours now- but I've got your money, so it's too late!) and I have written this chapter to document what a typical life for a modern fish frier might have been like. Most of us come from a family business or self made "one man band" background. I am confident that most fish friers will see elements of my story that mirror theirs and, although it may never help historians in years to come figure out why fish and chips was so popular, I hope you will be able to see where my enthusiasm for fish and chips comes from..

I was born in 1971, three years after my father started his career as a fish frier - renting his first shop in Shepherds Bush in North London. He was born in Cyprus and had come to England with many of his friends seeking their fortunes. This makes me typical of many second generation fish friers today. The number of Bubbles (affectionate Cockney rhyming slang for Greeks – bubble and squeak) who ended up as fish friers in the sixties and seventies was no coincidence. The allure of more modern western cultures and the promise of regular employment and easy money saw them coming over in their droves. Women like my mother simply couldn't resist their smouldering dark looks and charm - even though my old chap could barely speak the lingo.

When I came along, I was the fourth and last born. My brother was two years older and my sisters older still. It has often been joked that my very existence hinged on the fact that having four children excluded my father from national service back in Cyprus but I have never been able to confirm the truth of this.

Mark's father, Stavros Petrou

In those three years between my father entering the trade and my arrival, my father had gone from taking £68.00 (he remembers this was his first week's takings) to having saved a deposit to buy his first freehold shop in Brockley in South East London. All four kids and my folks lived above the Brockley shop in a two bed flat and although I possess one colour photo of me in a little blue pedal car in the back yard of the shop, memories of the rest of my time there are a bit sketchy. I have been reliably informed by my own mother that I used to chew on spare rib bones for hours when teething, although my earliest memories of being in and around fish and chip shops aren't until we moved out of London when I was four years old to Ramsey in Cambridgeshire in 1975.

Life in the fish and chip trade for this small child was fairly good. Our shop in Ramsey was comfortable. My brother and I shared a bedroom and it was right above the frying range and serving area. When it was bed-time, the warmth and smell from below and the hum of the extractor fan along with the muffled conversations between server and customer became a familiar lullaby that usually made me succumb to sleep easily. To me the smell of a fish and chip shop was what my home smelled like. I had a genuine interest from a young age about the trade and I asked probably far too many questions. Our fish at this time came in every other day, fresh, packed in ice and in wooden crates.

To me, the smell of a fish and chip shop was what my home smelled like

My mother used these crates for kindling and I can still vividly picture her breaking them across her knee in the morning and using newspaper rolled up and twisted into rings as a potent combination for getting the coal fire going in the sitting room.

I remember quite clearly how uncomplicated my life was back then and how I would be placed on the highest pile of sacks of potatoes with no chance of escape whilst Mum or Dad prepared the day's chips.

In Ramsey there were three fish and chip shops. Two were on opposite sides of the main street - my Dad's being the most popular - the third serviced a council estate round the back streets away from the shops. This was also owned by Bubbles - a nice family but, remarkably, not one of my Dad's cousins! The year after we arrived, the butcher's shop next door to the chippy closed and it was rumoured to have been bought by a Chinese family. They proposed to open a takeaway which angered my Father considerably. He approached the butcher who confirmed that he had indeed been approached but that he had not yet closed the deal.

My father went to the bank, had a cup of tea with the Manager and borrowed £3,000 there and then. He still owns that shop today and gets a good rental income from it. Within five years he had bought the chip shop across the road, too. On Sundays my father used to spend what seemed like forever laying out the week's takings on the kitchen table, counting it and then scribbling stuff down and then counting it again, then again, then again.

FISH & CHIPS - A NATIONAL TREASURE

In 1977 it was the Queen's Silver Jubilee year. Maybe it was my age, but the whole nation seemed to go far more nuts for this than it ever did for the fifty year celebration in 2002. I remember Union Jacks absolutely everywhere. There were street parties and for a six year old such a fantastic sense of celebration and excitement over something I didn't really understand at the time. On the 150th anniversary of fish and chips I would love to re-create, just for one day, a similar carnival atmosphere in my own community to mark the occasion.

Being at school and your Dad owning the local chippy was totally cool. Friends always wanted to come round for tea and in many ways I got to see a lot of my mum and dad because they worked so near. As I got older, though, we had our kitchen and sitting room taken from us to make way for a sit down area for customers. At this time I remember being aware of other types of fast food emerging. Wimpy was a big name and was being advertised on TV by Muhammad Ali. Kentucky Fried Chicken was also a name I remember too.

We got our first colour TV when we lived above that shop in Ramsey. Our family car was a metallic brown Ford Granada like the Sweeney's and the one in Blur's "Park Life" video. Every now and then on a Sunday, Mum and Dad would take all four of us kids and go down the A10 into North London to see either Uncle Andy or Uncle George or Uncle Costa - who were not real uncles but dad's best mates who all came to England at the same time and who all owned fish and chip shops. Us four were often left alone in that car for literally hours at a time. It was a different

The Petrou family shop in Chatteris, bought by Stavros in 1984

FISH & CHIPS - A NATIONAL TREASURE

world back then and although we were bored out of our minds we were never really in any danger. If we were well behaved we would get to go inside and play with our respective cousins in the backs of their chip shops. Some Mondays, my uncles might come up from London and go shooting for pheasants or pigeons with my Dad on a local friendly farmer's land

In 1980 my father and mother afforded themselves a proper family home. A nice three bed semi-detached house in the next village. From this point forward, Dad became more of a stranger who was either at work or asleep on the sofa on Sundays. The hours involved in running a fish and chip business are incredible. When you live where your folks work, you don't appreciate just how many hours they spend on their feet every single day. Now somewhat detached from seeing this - I began to appreciate just how hard they worked, although it wasn't until nearly a quarter of a century later when I became a parent myself that I realised just who they were working so hard for and why. At the time I almost resented my parents, and in my naïve head was convinced they wanted money more than they wanted to be with me. I have since made my peace with them and have thanked them publicly for the start in life they gave me.

Summers were spent on the Isle of Sheppey in Kent - Leysdown to be precise - in a caravan with my siblings and my Nan. It meant my folks could work without worry or distraction and we got to go cockling and spend our daily quid in the arcades whilst my Nan played Bingo. We often had fish and chips at the seaside (let's be honest, who didn't?) and the shop there was always packed. I always felt guilty eating someone else's other than my Dad's fish and chips but at the same time it felt right that I should test them in order to keep my faith and it was almost a comfort when they didn't measure up.

I got my first job as a spud boy aged thirteen - and went to my Dad's shop straight from school every day to peel and chip for that evening's trade. My friend Richard (who ended up a school teacher) used to help me. It was in that same spud room that I'd been in as a child with my folks that I began my career in the fish and chip trade. In 1984 my father bought what was eventually going to be crowned "best fish and chip shop in the land" and the site that I would invest over 25 years of my life into. The shop was in West Park Street in Chatteris and belonged to Pete Gowler. For the first few years Dad didn't even change the name above the door. By now, the years of being on his feet were starting to take their toll and his back was beginning to suffer, causing him a lot of pain. Locals were impressed by the quality of my father's fish and chips and he developed quite a following.

My big brother, who was a committed saver, had started his City and Guilds 706 1 and 2 in General Catering and was training to become a chef.

Father took me to Chatteris for the first time and I tried some fish and chips. This was the first time I had ever eaten them cooked in beef dripping. I was an instant convert and began to ask questions about the other shop in Ramsey and why it tasted so different over there. I remember Dad saying "You are more likely to be successful if you sell what people want to buy" and quite simply he meant that although there were only a few miles between Chatteris and Ramsey, there was a world of difference in tastes and he had been careful to pay attention to what locals preferred in each town - this is the fundamental core of the success of our nation's network of independent chip shops. In Ramsey it was groundnut oil and in Chatteris it was beef dripping. Although they were only 12 miles apart, there seemed to be decades between these two towns. Ramsey was just that bit nearer to a train station and the A1, which had attracted Londoners to the town. Chatteris was buried deeper into the Fens and more people still rode bicycles and wore practical clothing. There was more of a community in Chatteris and the local economy was driven by local employment, whereas in Ramsey, people commuted to work. Most folk knew each other in Chatteris and knew each other's business. I am not suggesting that Chatteris was old fashioned or backward – it was just different, in a nice way.

By 1987 my father was done in. Both daughters were married off and the nest was half empty. He had succumbed to diabetes and was now insulin-dependent and his back was pretty much spent, having done a lifetime's work in only forty-odd years. That year I left school and my brother - newly qualified as a chef - bought the family home from my parents and took over the shop in Chatteris. Sharing the same Christian name with Pete Gowler, the decision was made to call the shop Pete's Chip Shop. My folks decided to seek out warmer climates to ease their aching bones and moved back to Cyprus to retire on the rental income they were enjoying.

Aged sixteen, I took up residence in the house on the side of the chippy and took myself off to college to do business studies full time, as well as working in the shop evenings and weekends to help out. So many hours were spent either cutting fish or peeling spuds! Family life had pretty much dissolved, but I was disciplined enough to start and complete two years at college to achieve a National Diploma in Business Studies and get myself a place at Thames Polytechnic (now re-named Greenwich University). Law and Marketing were my favourite subjects and even living and studying in London did not prevent me from making the train journey back every Friday afternoon to Chatteris to help my brother out over the weekend in the chippy.

I lasted about a year at University. I decided that I had absorbed all that I could in a classroom and was finished with the education system. I knew already that I wanted a career in fish and chips but I took a few months off and moved up to Leeds with a couple of mates to sample northern hospitality and sell vacuum cleaners door to door. It was in Leeds at this time that I experienced severe financial hardship for the first time and also experienced the best fish and chips I have ever tasted in my life. The shop that sold them to me was about the size of a domestic single car garage and was a few doors away from the Tommy Wass pub on Dewsbury Road. The batter was really dark brown but incredibly delicate and had taken the full flavour of the hard-worked beef dripping it had been tempered in. When it broke, a contrast of virgin white flakes of haddock appeared, caressed by ghosts of steam. The smell of the malt vinegar seemed to intensify when sprinkled over the sizzling fish and took the air from my lungs for a moment. They sold a bread cake with an obscene amount of real butter on it and I swear that the resulting fish butty really was totally amazing.

After my sabbatical in Leeds, I embarked on what I would describe as my serious career in the fish and chip trade. As a local community chippy in a small rural market town, we were becoming aware of the influx of new food offers entering the high street. When my father

Mark (left) and Pete outside the family shop in West Park St, Chatteris

bought the shop in Chatteris in 1984, there were only a handful of other takeaways, but it seemed that now, whenever a shop became vacant, it re-opened as another fast food offering. I remember discussing at the time what our options might be and we explored expanding the menu - but my father wasn't keen.

In my youth I had often seen my father go off once a month to local meetings of the Peterborough branch of fish friers that was affiliated to the National Federation. He mixed in good company – in particular Martin Bunning (above) and Steve Goodacre who were previous winners of the coveted Fish and Chip Shop of the Year competition. I recall very vividly seeing the shiny trophy at their shop "Skippers" on Lincoln Road and dreamed of one day winning it myself. My brother and I had taken over membership when our Dad retired and we decided it was time to start taking an active interest in branch activities and so we started going to regular meetings too.

My brother and I, along with two other shop owners, organised a competition in the local paper for 24 independent fish and chip shops – all members from the Peterborough area. It involved a Spot-the-Difference challenge for kids, who could win the chance to be "Gladiators" for the day, representing their local chippy at an event staged at the local Ice Rink. We hired the venue, put a huge carpet over the ice and booked two well known TV personalities from London Weekend Television who were real life Gladiators from the popular TV series. This was probably the largest promotion ever to be successfully executed by a group of independent retailers in our trade and I believe to date, apart from radio promotions, it has never been repeated.

After putting in some pretty incredible hours over the next few years (most weeks we would notch up more than 100 hours each in the shop!) we saved hard and decided it was time to revamp our menu, refit our shop and relaunch our brand. In 1993 we took delivery of our five pan Florigo Dutch frying range, gave the whole shop a complete make-over and re-named it Petrou Brothers.

Armed now with renewed enthusiasm for fish frying and having gained the marketing background from further and higher education, along with Peter's underpinning catering knowledge and cooking skills, we began to build the brand that earned us a reputation for miles and miles around. We started to hold regular staff meetings to try and instill professional pride into our workforce and raise standards even higher. We set about compiling a training manual with everyone's input, so that future staff members could benefit from our expertise.

...most weeks we would notch up more than 100 hours each in the shop...

We embarked on a sustained marketing and PR campaign and introduced various loyalty schemes as a way of building in value to every customer's experience. Now irreversibly retired and sitting on a beach, our father offered very little resistance to menu changes. My brother and I began to enjoy very good levels of trade, considering the amount of new food offers entering the market place. We were well conditioned to the long hours and complete lack of any sort of social life and were single minded in our quest for fish frying fame and fortune.

1996 and there were now about seven takeaways in town, two fish and chips, two Chinese, two chicken and burger and one Tandoori. We had also expanded and bought our second shop in a village seven miles away called Somersham. At this time, I couldn't imagine having more than two shops. Only having one brother along with the understanding that it takes literally years to perfect and polish one's frying skills, I thought that I was reaching my full career potential. My brother went off to run the new shop and I remained at Chatteris. We had started selling kebabs in order to keep a hold of our market share, as there was only so much money to go round and we wanted to give our customers more than one reason to visit us. At this time, it proved to be a successful move and we also started making fresh dough on-site and installed a pizza oven, too. Although our reputation was still for our superb fish and chips, we made sure that our other products were of the same high standard. As the fast food market continued to grow, fish and chip sales seemed to remain steadfast rather than grow, with demand from customers who seemed to be expanding their culinary repertoires.

I had learned from the Fish Friers Review about a competition called Young Fish Frier of the Year. It was launched by Drywite Ltd and it showcased and encouraged new talent in the trade under the age of thirty. I naturally entered, as I quickly realised the potential benefits that this could bring to my business. I was really rather pleased when, to my complete surprise, I progressed through the rounds and into the final six in the country.

I genuinely enjoyed my job and took tremendous pleasure from the wonderful impromptu compliments that I would receive over the counter. At around the same time that I was enjoying my new found local celebrity status, I took on a lad part time to help me on Fridays and Saturdays called Ian Kilby. Ian was fifteen and not quite sure what he was going to do with his life and although he was well adjusted and popular outside of work, he found Petrou Brothers to be a fun, challenging and welcoming place to spend his time and earn money. I didn't win the competition and to be quite honest I didn't deserve to – within three years, however, Ian became the youngest ever person to this day to lift that trophy.

Ian Kilby, Young Fish Frier of the Year 2001

It is very rare for a boss to ever find a member of staff who cares and thinks more about the job than he does himself. I am often astounded by the level of commitment than Ian Kilby gave to his job in what were meant to be the most carefree years of anyone's life.

If ever there were to be a third Petrou Brother, I would have adopted him as my own flesh and blood. Working for wages, he became a silent hero when we entered Petrou Brothers in the UK Fish and Chip Shop of the Year Competition for the first time in 2000. You see, Ian is a Virgo, which makes him a perfectionist. His eye for detail and his determination for everything to be as good as it possibly could be allowed us to literally barge our way through every round and into the final Top Ten shops at the very first attempt. The shop looked great, the fish and chips tasted great and the staff were as motivated and passionate about serving the public as any group of individuals that I have ever seen anywhere. I honestly thought I could not lose.

I lost.........

Les Manning from Crewe served up his brand of what it takes to be a Champion and I returned home disappointed for my staff but again, my efforts had been noted and my genuine love of the trade itself was becoming virtually impossible for anyone in the business who met me to ignore.

I continued to take an active role at the NFFF in Peterborough and wrote articles for the Fish Friers Review in the hope of sparking some enthusiasm from fellow operators in sharing promotional ideas and getting together as a common marketing force. These efforts were often met with silence and I took comfort from the comradeship I had come to enjoy locally from fellow friers at the branch, who were just as keen as me to pool resources and promote as a united front for the benefit of fish and chips. I was starting to become well known within the trade now and at the time I didn't realise that this was having a positive impact on my business, too. It is not often considered but it's clearly a fact that all shops share customers. Whether it's visiting a loved one, a business trip or a holiday migration – whatever the reason, folk go travelling and when they do they still like their fish and chips.

Now when my customers were visiting other parts, and the shop owner asked them where they were from, it was becoming more and more regular for that frier to know my shop or my name and discuss my good reputation with the visiting punter. They would then return and tell me about how my name (or fame – delete as appropriate) was beginning to spread. This encouraged me even more. It was like giving honey to a bear.

> *It is very easy to be consumed by the day to day running of a fish and chip shop, almost like a hamster in a wheel...*

For the next few years, I focused on my love affair with fish and chips – at the expense of a couple of intimate relationships and the feelings of other people who really deserved better. It is very easy to be consumed by the day to day running of a fish and chip shop, almost like a hamster in a wheel. Every new day brings new challenges and by the time you have found solutions, you are starting the next new day. Although the routine of prepping spuds and cutting fish followed by service and then an hour or so in the afternoon to go to the bank and phone suppliers and then service again followed by cleaning down and going home seems to be repetitive, there is always a piece of equipment that needs a repair or a menu item that is unpredictably

Mark and his father photographed with chef Brian Turner

popular and suddenly you haven't get enough stock, or a member of staff lets you down and this will mean you are constantly battling to run at full strength. There is always the dangling carrot of a real sense of achievement in this job that keeps the donkey moving forward. In some ways, the role of boss can often be a thankless task, too. I like to think of my shop as the swan on the surface of the water, gliding gracefully, appearing beautiful and pleasing to the spectator/customer. The boss is the ugly orange feet pedalling furiously out of sight to keep the magic afloat...

I continued to make friends in the trade and developed a deeper understanding of the whole supply chain. Being the last person before the consumer, it is very easy to make assumptions about your raw materials and how they make their journey to your back door. We all appreciate the value we add to it as it passes through our business and out the front door but I do not think enough people really take the time to make the journey backwards to source. I have already mentioned several times in this chapter how my feelings towards fish and chips seemed to grow and to me it had been a constant, reliable feature in my life. Up to this moment in my career though, I will freely admit that my motivation and drive had been quite selfish. Meeting other professionals in the trade that contributed - be it wholesaler, manufacturer, farmer or fisherman - gave me a wider perspective and a whole new view point that thumped home to me the fact that almost every one connected to fish and chips was really very passionate about it. Now don't get me wrong, I am not going to try and convince you that anyone did their particular job for love – we all know that love doesn't pay the bills - but I found real characters everywhere I went, who all seemed to be in the business for something more than just wages.

The fishermen, for example, who risk their lives every single day that they go to work, have often taken over from their fathers, who in turn took over from their fathers before them. The farmer who, although extremely knowledgeable and hard working, relies on knowledge, luck and good weather to produce his crop. The batter manufacturers and indeed even the wholesalers or equipment suppliers were also second or third generation operators who had been in the trade since the early days. Every single one of them had challenges of their own.

As a younger frier who was always pleased to hear their stories, I found favour with many and began to amass a new type of wealth in the form of friendship. By understanding that they relied on my success for their livelihood too, I also developed a new sense of responsibility to do the job right and whenever a conversation with other friers took place regarding a price increase or poor service from further down the line, I

found myself more prepared to appreciate the perspective of the other guy and reason with my fellow fish frier rather than just agree. I think this is the turning point in my story that took me from good enough to make the finals in big competitions to being ready to truly represent my industry. From then on, I always felt that winning Fish and Chip Shop of the Year would not be about what I could take from the title but what I might be able to bring to it.

I met my future wife Clare who decided that I was the one for her – and before I could mount any sort of defence or come to my senses it was too late. I was off the market. She was extremely beautiful (still is) and I gave her a job until she left to go travelling around Canada. We

married in 2003 and she began her career as a legal secretary/actress (whenever there was work) and continued to help out in the shop, too. In February 2005 we were blessed with the arrival of baby Madeleine. The instinct to provide kicked in, I guess, and I stepped back a little from the front line and began to focus more on working smart rather than working hard.

I got invited to the 2005 Fish and Chip shop of the Year finals in January 2006 as a guest of a sausage manufacturer. I had already started making plans for a community website and wanted to speak to as many industry leaders as possible. The occasion was the perfect environment to drum up support. I had recognised that as a network of independent retailers, we all face the same challenges, threats and opportunities.

Historically, fish friers had always demonstrated the most comradeship at events hosted by the National Federation of Fish Friers. However in more recent times, there had been a growing trend for membership of the NFFF to be taken directly with head office and this resulted in the closure of many local branches (with the exception of my local branch in Peterborough and a few others).

My idea was to create an "on-line" environment where friers could meet up for free (or the cost of their internet connection) when their loved ones were tucked up in bed or at a time convenient to them and basically talk shop. I pitched my idea to the top brass in the business and they seemed very enthusiastic.

Nigel and Linda Hodgson lifted the Trophy that day and became the best friers in the land. They are a lovely couple and were so very

deserving. Seeing their pure delight and the admiration they enjoyed from so many accomplished professionals within the industry was like a final call at the departure gate to destiny for me and I decided there and then that the next year was going to be my year. Simple as that...

Within two months I had coordinated a complete makeover of my Chatteris store, including the latest Florigo HE pan technology from Holland, and launched www.chippychat.co.uk - the first and only forum for fish friers. It featured a news page, a links page to other relevant sites connected to the trade and a live community with more than a dozen open forums for people to start new threads in and get talking.

Within four months. I had over 1000 members, nearly 500 live topics and was receiving 50,000 unique hits a month. The wealth of knowledge and the access to literally hundreds of years of experience empowered every single person who joined up and joined in. I had decided to self fund the enterprise but now there was an orderly queue forming of suppliers who wanted to have a presence on the site because they could see the benefits of being on board before their competitors were – most suppliers, though, joined up and lurked around the forums, scared to contribute preferring to observe what friers were talking about.

It was the end of June 2006 and the refurbishment had been completed at Chatteris a month earlier. The first round of judging for Fish and Chip Shop of the Year had begun and I took the opportunity to mark the occasion with an official reopening of the shop. It also happened to be our 25th anniversary and not being one to miss a trick when it comes to PR (my new motto now being "If you don't tell you won't sell!") I invited celebrity chef Brian Turner to come to the shop and help us celebrate.

Brian Turner (affectionately shortened to BT by most) is a true Yorkshireman who loves to celebrate all things British and edible. He carries with him at all times his own silver chip fork – such is his love for our nation's favourite meal. I did not know at the time, but our paths would cross several times in the future, and I must make a passing comment about his genuine warmth and the kindness he afforded me in my attempts to be a champion fish frier. His visit was timely and it gave my staff and my customers a real sense of purpose and belief that we could actually be the best fish and chip shop in the UK, even though we were a small takeaway, seventy miles from the coast in a Fenland market town.

We sailed through the first round, which involved 300 nomination forms from the public, and were one of the top ten shops in our geographical region which was Cambridgeshire, Rutland and Lincolnshire.

The really fantastic thing about the Fish and Chip Shop of the Year competition is that it drives up standards. It forces everyone that enters

Mark (right) and Pete with Mark's wife Clare on their win in January '07

to take a good hard look at their operation and try to improve it. The real winners are the customers, because they get better service, cleaner shops and tastier meals. The criteria that you are assessed on mean that no stone is left unturned. Your hygiene practices, cooking techniques, due diligence, paper work, service procedures, environmental policies and legal compliance are all scrutinised. Any shop that progresses - or for that matter can achieve the Seafish Quality Award (not a competition but a recognised Industry standard qualification) - demonstrates the very highest levels in all the places the customer doesn't get to see, as well as front of house. This competition really sorts the wheat from the chaff. It is extremely demanding and very, very thorough.

Arrogant as it may sound, having shed the blood, sweat and tears myself, I was not surprised when we were announced as the winner for the Area and beat the other area finalist after that. We were short listed in the final ten shops in the UK and given our second opportunity to go to London.

This time felt different to the first time we made the finals. I wrote my presentation in a matter of minutes. It briefly explained my journey in the trade and honestly laid down why I wanted to be top chip champ. I delivered it to a panel of industry experts without nerves or expectation and thoroughly enjoyed the whole experience.

I took the word champion literally, and decided to make my year count by "championing" fish and chips

Winning was a very humbling experience. Putting Anstruther Fish Bar into second place (they later went on to win in 2008) and beating the other eight finalists was no mean feat because of the high standards that they all set. It is only after winning the title of UK Fish and Chip Shop of the Year that you begin to realise what an important role you

Above: Mark, Pete and Ainsley Harriott on Ready, Steady Cook, and below, Mark and Barry Norman launch Barry's pickled onion range

have to perform for the whole industry. I took the word champion literally and decided to make my year count by "championing" fish and chips. It's like wearing two different hats – on the one hand, showing the industry how to raise standards and move forward and on the other, promoting fish and chips to the buying public.

I seized this opportunity with both hands, appearing on Ready Steady Cook, the Alan Titchmarsh show and BBC World News to name just a few. I used the platform to highlight just how far the industry has come, talking about how cod is sourced responsibly, the low fat content of fish and chips and what fantastic value for money it still represents. Winning gave me something with which I could repay my loved ones and customers for their unwavering support. It put the sleepy town of Chatteris firmly on the map, making it a magnet for fish and chip lovers everywhere. People made special journeys from as far afield as New Zealand and the United States of America just to sample our fish and chips, and other businesses in the town prospered as a direct result of this. It was a truly special time in my life, for it coincided with the arrival of my second daughter, Imogen.

I took to writing again (something I had been known to do from time to time) for Seafish, and several trade magazines. My monthly columns were well read and I often found myself recognised whenever I attended trade shows and other industry events. I found the whole thing quite flattering but didn't really take the celebrity thing seriously at all. My learning curve accelerated steeply due to the intense and knowledgeable company I was keeping. Requests to consult began to trickle in at first and then flow quite quickly and all of a sudden my expertise suddenly had a value. I found myself working with other fish friers and real celebrity chefs with Michelin stars who were all desperate to learn my techniques. I became more of a diplomat and my confidence grew in public speaking and then my year at the top was over in a flash.

The new champ was a really nice guy: Gordon Hillan of the Townhead Café in Biggar. He and his missus, Sandra, a lovely lass, were both deserving champions. Nonetheless, I was frustrated that my title had gone to Scotland, because I had only just got my teeth into the job of championing fish and chips, and now had to stand aside.

But the competition rules do not allow for a champion to defend their crown, and although I felt like there was unfinished business there was nothing I could have done about it. I entered again once my imposed exile from the competition was over and guess what.. I made it into the final ten again. Not only did I make the final for Fish and Chip Shop of the Year, I also made the final for two other awards as well: the Staff Training and Development Award, plus the Heinz sponsored "PleazMe!" award for customer service.

No one had ever lifted the crown twice in the twentyone years of the competition's history. No one still has, for it was not meant to be.

Top to bottom: Scotland the Brave - Mark's successors as winners of the National Fish & Chip Shop of the Year Title:
Gordon and Sandra Hillan of the Townhead Cafe, 2007: Robert and Alison Smith of the Anstruther Fish Bar, 2008; the Fionda family of Atlantic Fast Food, 2009/10

The very people that I had beaten into second place the year I lifted the title - Robert and Alison of the Anstruther Fish Bar - won and took the trophy back to Scotland for the second year in a row. The following year the title went to Scotland for the third time in succession, this time to the Fionda's of Atlantic Fast Food in Coatbridge.

I have since opened another three shops - nearly going broke and insane in the process. The town I had invested more than a quarter of a

"...two amazing daughters..." - Madeleine and Imogen on the beach

century of my life into feeding broke my heart. A really poor imitation of my award winning shop opened just a few hundred yards from me. They offered big portions for less money but ignored all the ethical practices that I employed. My hard work, my dedication and my commitment to my community meant nothing. I employed local people, supported local initiatives and losing just one single customer to a shop that really only wanted to cash in on my success and take money out of the local economy was almost too much for me to comprehend. I prefer to work any other shop than the one I own in Chatteris these days, although trade there is still very brisk. At the start of this chapter there was so little competition. Now we have fourteen takeaways in a town that has grown very little since my story began.

I am today active as a newly elected executive councillor for the National Federation of Fish Friers and continue to consult and write. Yet still, though I am father to two amazing daughters and husband to an incredibly talented wife - who is winning national awards in her own field as a radio broadcaster - I cut fish every day and continue to fry in all of my shops as often as my diary will permit. As a bare minimum, that has to be every Friday and Saturday, day and night, because I still cannot resist the *buzz* of a busy shift!

Chapter Four – the four corners of the circle

If you've ever wondered – how does that work? Or where did that come from? Then you probably still won't find the answers in this chapter. In its 150 years, the fish and chip industry has survived being born into poverty, two world wars and countless attacks of slander. Along the way it has been shaped and revolutionised by events, innovators and unsung heroes. I have commented already that the fish and chip industry is a special trade to belong to because of the passion and the unique individuals that are the very fibres that knit together to form the fabric of the frying community. This chapter celebrates four of the most pivotal contributions that allowed the industry to evolve to the monumental heights it has so far reached. I could write about many more and I know there will be some who would have liked to have read different tales than the ones I have chosen to tell. Hard luck again – write your own book – these are the ones that made the grade for me…sorry Uncle Arthur – you deserve to be in here too, but I did your beloved Federation instead…

First corner

The decision to put finger to keyboard and commit my thoughts to text came about after reading a book titled "The Fish Frier and his Trade." It is an incredibly detailed account of the early mechanics of an industry that fuelled my desire to be an achiever in both labour and life. It is a very rare book indeed and was gifted to me by an extremely passionate and successful fish and chip purveyor from Wells next the Sea – Marcus French of French's Fish and Chips. The author of the book called himself "Chatchip". Having set up an online community for fish friers called Chippychat.co.uk only 12 months before, I was intrigued to find out more about the man known as "Chatchip" – his legacy is the one of the cornerstones that helped form the foundations of the thriving industry we all enjoy today as both customer and operator.

"Chatchip" was a man called William Loftas. He demonstrates a depth of knowledge in his book that defies belief. He was a man much my superior, in that he could fill a book - three times the number of pages with text half the size - all about an industry half the age of the one I

write about today. Not only that, but his book was crammed full of pure facts. His research and considered opinion must surely have taken as long to give to the interested world as it did to experience it all. Unfortunately it did not fly off the shelves and very few copies remain. It is an absolute must for the fish frying anorak and not designed at all to openly share and entertain like my little book, but rather educate its audience. Loftas did far more for fish and chips than leave an obscure nom de plume text book, though. He is quite rightly referred to these days as "The Father of the Federation."

With an industry firmly established and having reached its half century, William Loftas was the man who was able to persuade seventeen different fish friers' organisations to meet at the Albion Hotel in Manchester on the 11th November 1913 and create a National Federation of Fish Friers – capable of being both a champion and protector of the interests of friers for an affiliation fee of just one shilling per year. Prior to this event, the industry had never had a voice and was never really taken seriously or considered important at national level. William Loftas gave the industry that platform and I am delighted to spend the next few pages highlighting 97 years of significant contributions, history and achievements that have proven time and time again how important a role the NFFF has played in safeguarding fish friers' livelihoods and rights. From its very conception, the NFFF stood up for the rights of its members and although in its acorn days, numbers were only in their hundreds, negotiations with the Government during the First World War over shortages of raw materials, along with imposed curfews, saw membership reach 3,000 in under six years by 1919.

By the time World War Two arrived, the NFFF had over 10,000 members, peaking at 10,914 in 1947

In 1925 the NFFF launched its own magazine titled the The National Caterers Review – it was to change its name to the Fish Friers Review in 1928 and has served to this day as a provider of information, companionship and sense of community for generations of members. During the late 1930's and early 40's the Federation proved invaluable by corresponding secretly with the Ministry of Agriculture and Fisheries, securing and preserving raw materials for its members. Price controls on white fish were introduced in June 1941 and ended in April 1950. By the time World War Two arrived the NFFF had over 10,000 members, peaking at 10,914 in 1947. The Federation continued to fight for its members as white fish prices began to rise. The Government formed the White Fish Authority in 1950 coinciding with the end of pricing controls and the NFFF battled on behalf of its members to have the authority abolished (it eventually was disbanded and replaced by the Seafish Industry Authority in 1981). The NFFF was there again in 1955 and 1957, winning concessions for its members when the Food Hygiene Regulations and Shops Bill were introduced and threatening fair play and friers' interests.

In the late 1950's the NFFF started to broker discounts on paper and other raw materials for its members as well as saving many businesses from certain peril by securing potato imports after the poor harvest of 1957. A Government enquiry exploring the fishing industry in 1959 saw the NFFF provide evidence that resulted in a Federation fish scheme for members being introduced providing another great benefit. In 1965, the Federation presented the Malin family with a plaque celebrating 100 years of fish and chips – citing them after 18 months of searching as the oldest fish and chip shop in the world, although the NFFF later accepted that 1860 was the more likely date that the oldest shop in the world was established. In 1967 and again in 1969 there was a shortage of potatoes and cod and haddock and once again the Federation achieved imports for its members. Decimalisation in 1971, the introduction of VAT in 1973, the Cod Wars and droughts in 1972, 1975 and 1976 along with battles over opening times and campaigning for increased planting of potatoes demonstrates time and time again why our network of independent fish and chip shop owners needs representation at the very highest level.

Fighting against the introduction of VAT on takeaway food by delivering a petition to government with over one million signatures on it. The introduction of City and Guilds in Fish Frying Practice qualifications. Assistance with tax investigations. Discounted insurance and energy provider schemes. Employment law and health and safety protection schemes. These are just some of the benefits enjoyed in my time as a member - and let's not forget Enterprise Awards, NVQs, and the Training School at Head Office with the eternally youthful Arthur Parrington (who also gave his time and considerable wealth of knowledge to this chapter) and all the steering committees that the NFFF sits on to continually help shape the future of the trade for both

celebrating

150

—— years of ——

FISH'N'CHIPS

1 8 6 0 - 2 0 1 0

still the Nation's favourite!

its members and the frying community at large. Then of course there are the 150 year celebrations. Do I need to go on?

Yes, I do, because there's potentially a sad ending to the story…

> *An industry without a voice - especially one as fragmented as ours - can quickly plunge into chaos*

Throughout the Federation's colourful existence, it has always had changeable membership numbers. The importance of its existence has never been in doubt. In fact, as you read the last couple of pages, you can really get a feel for just how much the Federation has done and still continues to do on ehalf of all friers – not just the ones who pay subscriptions - and there's the rub. There are, of course, benefits to membership but in the past, friers have wanted to belong to the Federation because they saw the need to be united and represented at national level. Nowadays, fish friers see a subscription to the NFFF as an unnecessary expense. Maybe it's because the high street now has operators in direct competition with each other; perhaps it's because independent retailers are worrying more about issues closer to home - like staffing - than the general threats to the industry like fishing quotas and changes in legislation. Whatever it is, membership figures are lower than I would like them to be. An industry without a voice – especially one as fragmented as ours in the diversity of its operators - can quickly plunge into chaos. In my opinion, the Federation deserves its subscription from every member of the frying community that gets to use the "Fish and Chips" brand for free. If every frier were to support the NFFF the way it used to in tough times, it will continue to provide a beacon of light for its members to follow. However, it does need to evolve.

Friers in 2010 have different needs to those one hundred years ago and the NFFF needs to get on board with this reality. Friers nowadays have access to literally decades of expertise through the Federation, along with the best training facilities in the world. The NFFF is not perfect, though. It is run by fish friers for fish friers. I am currently an executive councillor and have been looking very hard at the role the NFFF plays into today's market place. In 2010, for example, it brokered an exclusive deal for providing cheap energy for its members as well as a discounted insurance scheme. It co-ordinated efforts to celebrate 150 years of fish and chips by hosting talks with all the main industry organisations round the same table. The NFFF needs to appoint professionally trained staff to assume the key corporate roles in order to operate more professionally than it does at national level and perform more effectively for its members. In todays climate, corporate language is more formal and structured. A trade body like the NFFF needs to keep with the times and presently is failing on two counts. The first is the way it promotes what it does for its members. If you don't tell, you don't sell and the NFFF does a terrible job of getting the message out about all the valuable things it is still doing. The second is the way it continues to be run by great guys like me and Arthur Parrington who have all the passion in the world for our trade but don't really know how to chair a meeting or even put together resolutions or proposals in a language our potential new industry partners will understand and want to get on board with. We need to remedy this as soon as possible.

Looking forward, there is no doubt that the National Federation of Fish Friers will reach its hundredth birthday in 2013. I would like it go beyond that by offering even more services to its members, like a promotions club that designs and prints bespoke branded point of sale for its members, or exclusive deals on raw materials - again through its relationship with industry supply chains. More importantly, though, I want friers to understand just how big a setback to our industry it will be if the NFFF were to ever not exist. It will get better at promoting what it does because I will see to that and it will become more professional in the way it operates at national level because that is what it needs to do to deliver the best service it can to its members. All the members and non members need to do is perhaps look forward to the next shortage of spuds, exorbitant fish prices or threat to the industry and imagine that there is no one to help them through it. Maybe then they will realise that for the price of less than a portion of fish and chips a week, they will have all the support they need at their finger tips.

Second corner

Born in December 1918, Malcolm Charles Lee has without a doubt had an impact on your life. If you are a lover of fish and chips, you will not have been able to escape his contributions to the frying trade. He was just eight years old when his friend's parents converted the front room of their house into a fish and chip shop and his interest in the trade was ignited. He soon became fascinated by the whole operation and was always willing to help out. He learned the valuable lesson of hard work and when he left school

five years later in 1932 he had found a part time job with another local frier peeling potatoes.

As a reward for his efforts one day, Malcolm was permitted to take home some peeled potatoes for his mother to cook for lunch. She remarked how convenient it had been to get them in this prepared state and this comment prompted Malcolm, with his father H G Lee's help, to set up the Pioneer Potato Company to supply peeled spuds to homes in the local area. His father bought him a second hand potato peeler and a box-tricycle and he set up his operation in outbuildings behind the family home in Arthur Street in West Bromwich. Malcolm soon realised that there was a market for his wares, but he found that his efforts were hampered by the fact that he had to transport his prepared potatoes in water to prevent them from discolouring.

Malcolm and his father agreed that there must be a scientific solution to this problem. Malcolm set about overcoming it by enrolling on a chemistry course at Birmingham Technical College. He stayed after class one day to discuss the problem with the course lecturer and this sparked the lecturer's interest and he immediately took up the challenge. He came up with several suggestions that would all prevent discolouration but because of strict regulations that control the use of chemical additives, they - along with a total of thirteen different formulations - were rejected before a successful final family recipe was approved.

Within a year, Malcolm had employed two other boys with identical box-tricycles and in the winter months, Malcolm was approached serendipitiously by a fish frier whose water supply had frozen and needed Malcolm's services so that he could open his shop that evening. The frier – who was extremely grateful - noted that Malcolm's spuds did not discolour and this I feel was the pivotal eureka moment in this fascinating story. You see, Malcolm Lee was never going to be afraid to work extremely hard, but he was also a bright young man and he recognised that his magic formula had a potentially huge dormant market among the tens of thousands of fish and chip shops that were the length and breadth of the country and that they would all benefit from using it – they just didn't realise that it existed. It did not take long before friers were actively seeking Malcolm out.

In 1934 the Lee family opened their own fish and chip shop, to help them to fully understand and appreciate the needs of the market they were starting to supply with great success. His operation was beginning to outgrow the site in Arthur Street. This vital step gave Malcolm a practical environment in which to develop even more products for front-line fish friers including "Maltflaven" condiment essence. Maltflaven is the reason chip shop vinegar tastes better than any other vinegar you can buy anywhere else and it was one of many new products. It was the "Drywite" formula however that was capturing the attention of the whole frying community. The benefits of using this amazing product far exceeded what

Drywite became a must have product for fish friers

Malcolm had first set out to achieve, because not only did it allow chips to be transported without them turning pink or black, but also it allowed them to be drained well in advance of frying. This meant that frying times were greatly reduced because a dry chip will fry much quicker than a wet one. It also meant that frying temperatures would remain higher, resulting in less fat being absorbed, making healthier chips and the frying medium would last longer and remain in better condition through not having extreme temperature swings and excess contact with water. Not only that, but Drywite virtually disappears during the frying process making it morally the correct decision to use as well.

Drywite became a must have product for fish friers. In 1938 the limited company that had been formed several years earlier moved into new larger premises which Malcolm shared with the Lee family's engineering and haulage business. When the Second World War came along, the family business contributed to the war effort by manufacturing munitions and the production of Drywite was also maintained to help friers prevent the nation from starving.

Malcolm Lee made chips healthy. Malcolm Lee made chips better and Malcolm Lee never stopped looking to improve working standards, practices and conditions for people in the frying trade.

In the 1950's, for example – according to his son Kelvin Lee (now Managing Director) - Malcolm was aware that several friers had found themselves in trouble with health inspectors over the use of wooden barrels to treat and store their chips. He found a solution to the problem  at a manufacturing exhibition, in the form of polythene moulded baby baths. He enquired about having bespoke chip barrels made of the same material but was told that he would need to order 10,000 just to make tooling costs viable. Malcolm took the gamble and produced literature, not to preach to fish friers about the hygiene benefits, but for the health inspectors who then became a commission-free sales force as they showed them to every frier in their wards. He sold his 10,000 barrels within 12 months and millions more since… It was also early in this decade that the Drywite Corporation of America was set up by Malcolm to produce it over the pond under licence.

His daughter Briar joined the company in 1960 – the same year that the Drywite formula was first produced in powder form (now the company's best seller) and his son Kelvin followed a decade later in 1972. The company continued in the same vein, introducing more and more innovations to friers which ultimately benefited Joe Public too. Malcolm Lee officially retired in 1988 and Kelvin assumed the role of MD and Briar that of Sales and Marketing Director. Long before Mission Statements were called Mission Statements, Drywite Ltd had a work ethic that Malcolm himself describes in an article he penned for the Fish Friers Review shortly before his death in 1993. It reads "Caring sufficiently to recognise and answer the needs of the fish frying trade through close association beyond the limitation of financial reward." There has never been a more appropriate time in the history of puns

Briar Wilkinson of Drywite with Daniel Harding, the 2009-2010 winner of the Young Frier of the Year title, inaugurated by Briar and her brother Kelvin in memory of Malcolm Lee

to say that both Kelvin and Briar are chips off the old block. They have carried on their father's valuable work with tremendous enthusiasm and continue to contribute to the trade in ways many mathematicians or cut-throat city bankers would consider beyond charity and good financial sense. They do so because they are able to and because they have bucket loads of the same passion that I have described throughout the whole frying community in previous chapters.

In 1995 Drywite launched the Young Fish Frier of the Year Competition in memory of Malcolm Lee. By creating this accolade for younger friers, it has served to validate a career in the trade and recognises the potential of emerging talent at the same time. It has been an important stepping-stone in producing so many of the country's top shops and I am grateful not only for the support I have received from Drywite but for the friendship afforded to me by a company that never seems to lose momentum or resolve.

Third corner

Self-labelled the "Oliver Reed" of the frying trade, this was the only time I've ever heard Bill Shaw undersell anything. I doubt many could get this man to give up his time to actually lower his guard, be open and candid and in his own words describe his career. I think for both of us, it turned out to be a real treat. The time before he agreed to see me, he had been incredibly rude to me. It turns out, I'd actually hurt his feelings. Who'd have thought it? Bill Shaw has actually got feelings. He's a man with a reputation that has come at a price. I always considered him to be more like Marmite than Oliver Reed – you either love him or hate him. Oliver Reed was actually a really great actor who was unfortunately

judged more on his appalling off-screen performance than his thespian achievements.

Bill Shaw was the most amazing artist who forced people to challenge and question their own ideals and this often had abrasive but incredible results. Bill Shaw is responsible in some way, shape or form for helping to create most of the greatest shops and brands in our trade today. I am delighted to share his story and pay tribute to unquestionably the most successful salesman in the history of fish and chips. I am publicly sorry to have broken my word.

Bill Shaw was an only child born on Christmas Eve 1947 to Kate and Billy Shaw in Burnopfield, County Durham. His mother worked on the land and the buses and his father was a pitman. Billy had lost a leg during the Second World War and having been down the mine prior to being called up to serve his country, he now worked above ground issuing tokens to those working on the mine face below. A man of real character and charm. Bill remembers him as being incredibly well-liked and an extremely funny man with an ability to entertain by sharing anecdotes and telling jokes. Although Bill only had the influence of his father for twenty years before he passed away, he credits him for helping to forge a promising career for Bill on the stage from the age of just five years of age (up to the age of thirty). At 16 Bill left school and walked straight into a full time job at the local bank as a clerk. He hated it, found it soul destroying and after three long years he started his career as a salesman for Kleenex. "All salesman are successful failures," said Bill. He admits that it wasn't because he was an only child, nor was it a very Northern thing to become quite so nomadic, but Bill decided very early on in his career that he was ambitious and that his ambition would fuel the decision-making element of his career development, "You go wherever you needed to go." After Kleenex and the loss of his father, Bill worked at a crisp company next and quoted again "When you get a new job, you automatically think about the next one." Several jobs later, including a spell at Automatic Catering Supplies where he made Sales Director in 1983, Bill then gained the title of deputy managing director of a company called Colpac.

Colpac was a forty-year-old company specialising in packaging. Bill Shaw's appointment - having worked at ACS. - was to undertake the challenge of building a Fast Food Division for his new employer. At this time, the fast food market was exploding - in packaging terms as well as in diversification. The world was being led by the American market and cardboard packaging was very new in the UK and was only just being considered. By 1986 Bill had started to notice a small independent retailer in Wisbech - punching well above his weight in respect of the large volumes of cardboard boxes that were being ordered. Bill was intrigued by his customer's success and decided to investigate. It turned out this retailer was a fried fish and chip operation on Norfolk Street called Boyle's. What Bill discovered was a pioneer by the name of Chris Boyle. At face-value his shop appeared to be a very good example of a typical chippy. Well presented, cooking fresh food to order (not common practice in those days – especially in busy shops) and with an innovative approach to the merchandising of his takeaway meals. The jewel in the crown, though, was his frying range – not that Bill would have known this without Boyle pointing it out.

Boyle explained that the whole concept for frying had been turned on its head by the Dutch and that his frying range in this unassuming back street of a Fenland market town was in fact the first of its type in the UK. Boyle invited Bill Shaw to sell the ranges - but Bill was already way ahead of him on what he describes as "a sleeping giant that just needed stirring." He'd developed a complete arsenal of sales techniques over nearly twenty years and had also met and married Jean Davis – an accomplished and successful marketeer in her own right whom Bill had met during his time at Golden Wonder. Jean Shaw knew exactly how to raise awareness, build brands and create a profile. Bill considers her to be his secret weapon and is pleased to be able to recognise her as the real key to his success, They knew exactly what was required and Bill promptly handed in his notice, his car keys and the comfort of a very secure, well paid executive life style in exchange for a twelve month contract and a smile.

Bill set about selling not a frying range, but a dream. What Bill realised was that fish friers had a restrictive lifestyle. He developed a business concept around this new-fangled way of frying that promised friers a different and exciting way of running their businesses. This concept involved a complete refurbishment and forward-thinking approach to the whole operation that focused on making fish and chip shops look as though they were a part of a chain – giving them a corporate image like the American giants and offering the potential to standardise their operation and break free from the shackles that the highly-skilled job of frying had always locked to an owner/operator. The idea of owning a shop that rivalled the new types of food offers emerging was very attractive. Of course, the reality was a little flawed until the later evolution and arrival of high efficiency pan technology, but it was a giant step ahead of its rivals at the time and both Bill and Jean knew they could make everyone who would listen believe them.

The challenges of getting anyone to take them seriously and putting together a complete package proved to be minor compared to being able to move the project forward with Planet. Within six months the relationship began to sour. Planet ranges went no further than a handful of installations. A third party brought in to the Planet project as a technical advisor was a real gentleman by the name of Ray Claridge. He was a well-known and well-respected man, with an engineering background, who had serviced conventional frying equipment in the area for many years. Trustworthy and a man of integrity, Ray provided Bill with an opportunity to pursue his quest for fish frying domination by introducing him to another Dutch frying range manufacturer called Florigo. They left Planet and Chris Boyle behind and embarked on their quest to convert the frying community – one shop at a time.

Bill and Ray got six ranges installed in 1987 and Jean started to perform her magic. Bill joked "If I got lost on the way home from work, Jean got it in the newspaper!" She actively sought out new business by creating a presence in the market place and placing adverts and creating news stories about Florigo in the trade magazines. This was something UK range manufacturers had never really done. Buying a frying range was something almost formulaic, before Florigo. You simply bought the same range your father had had and his father before him and so on. They were all much of a muchness and performed the same role, except that you were used to what you were used to and so you didn't stray from that familiarity. Now, all of a sudden, there were all these stories and claims about this new kid on the block and what it was capable of doing. I remember hearing about round pans to cook chips in and square pans to cook fish in and thinking "Pah! That ain't ever gonna work!"

Bill had charisma and charm - but more importantly - Bill made friends with his leads, and they couldn't say no

Money was extremely tight for Florigo but thanks to Jean, they arrived with a helluva bang and established this huge presence in the market place almost overnight. Bill got to work straight away taking enquiries and courting potential customers with consideration and attention. Often he would take clients hundreds of miles to see shops who had installed one of his ranges – the client not realising that this was simply because that was where the nearest one was! Bill used the time during such journeys with clients to paint pictures with his words about how their shops would look and, of course, when they arrived at the refurbished shop with the Florigo range installed in it, the clients were usually blown away. Bill was slick. Bill had charisma and charm but - more importantly - Bill made friends with his leads and they couldn't say no. He made the purchase feel right and usually turnover went up dramatically as a result of Bill's influence.

This is an appropriate time for me comment that the food produced on those early ranges was usually of a superior quality and consistency

Lincolnshire Free Press, Tuesday, August 7, 1990   FLORIGO NEWS III

Florigo supplies Russian revolution

FLORIGO is responsible in part for a revolution in the fast food industry.

Bill Shaw explains: "We started to project the concept to the fish frying market about three years ago that they were missing the boat in terms of keeping up with other fast food operators.

"A survey by the sea fish industry confirmed that the British public's favourite fast food was fish and chips but asked what they thought about the average fish and chip shop the answer was not a lot.

"We have been trying to put this right since 1987 - by offering not just a superb, state of the art frying range but the opportunity to update the fish and chip shop image and compete with the likes of McDonalds, Kentucky Fried Chicken and pizza restaurants."

The Florigo range is manufactured in Holland by Florigo whose industrial wing makes commercial sized ranges for McDonalds, Kentucky Fried Chicken and Burger King.

In fact this part of the company has made equipment for the McDonald's store in Moscow.

But Bill is keen to emphasise that a range on its own will not turn a business round - the Florigo full treatment will.

"We say you can increase turnover from £1500 a week to £2,500 to £3,000. That is the sort of increase we get which of course increases the businesses asset base.

"Buy a shop for £100,000 - that's average for a shop going £1500 a week. Spend £40,000 on a revamp and increase the turnover to £3,000 and that will increase the value of the shop to £175,000 - the worth of a business is calculated from premises and turnover.

That means the businesses asset base had increased by £75,000." He gave examples of fish and chip shop owners like Harold and Pat Radford of Darwen, Lancashire, who bought their business two years ago for £45,000. They spent £36,000 and have almost

trebled the value of the business which now stands at £125,000. At another shop in Ruskington, the new owner increased trade from £1000 to £2,300 a week which he did not believe could be beaten.

Now, with the Florigo treatment, his weekly trade has jumped to between £4,500 and £5,000 a week.

"He says he just does not know where all the business has come from. He really believed he had reached saturation point and it was not possible to bring any more business in.

"He was doing 20 burgers a week - now he is doing 400.

Another fish and chip shop, Skippers at Peterborough, uses Florigo frying ranges and has been judged fish and chip shop of the year.

That competition was sponsored in part by Florigo and it was particularly pleasing for Bill Shaw to discover that three of the seven finalists had Florigo ranges and the winner, Skippers, was one of those.

MEET THE BOSS

Fish and chip shops have got to move with the times - and there is some catching up to do. But we have shown that, using the Florigo concept, they can be competitive. The Florigo concept has helped many increase turnover, even when they thought there could be no possibility of increase, and boost their asset base. Increases in turnover have been two and threefold.

BILL SHAW

NO PLACE LIKE HOME

GEORDIE Bill Shaw has been selling for 22 years - from Kleenex to Golden Wonder his career has revolved around some famous names.

Now he is involved with Florigo, a famous name in the frying industry, and he believes he has settled down....for now.

Work, promotion, ambition has kept Bill and his family on the move. He has been three years in his present home at Market Deeping - the

longest time in any one house over the last 12 years.

"I feel settled here now. It's a lovely part of the world, fabulous countryside, and the people are superb," said Bill...." "and the A1 is not far away," said the businessman inside him.

But he had assurances for local people and the business community that Florigo is established in Market Deeping despite the lure of big city business incentives.

THE TASTIEST FISH AND CHIPS IN THE UK - THAT'S THE PROUD BOAST OF FLORIGO EQUIPPED SKIPPERS OF PETERBOROUGH (SEASIDE FISH AND CHIPS IN TOWN).

VOTED THE UK'S BEST FISH & CHIP SHOP

FISH & CHIPS

FISH & CHIPS

SKIPPERS

FISH & CHIPS

SKIPPERS

PRODUCTS BY Kodak

Bill takes pride of place in an early edition of Florigo News

compared with fish and chips fried on traditional ranges of the time. This was no gimmick. The principle behind Dutch frying does give a frier the potential to produce consistently high quality meals. People who took the time to explore Bill's concept were usually sold on it straight away.

By 1987 Florigo had grown into a cleverly crafted front with a presence in the market place many times greater than its actual mass. By coincidence at this time, Bill was contacted by an old colleague who had worked with him and Jean at Golden Wonder in the Public Relations department called David Eames. Seafish had taken him on to help with their promotions and he had come up with the idea of running a national competition to showcase and promote the fish and chip sector. Bill was asked if Florigo would like to be the main sponsor of the first Fish and Chip Shop of the Year Competition. The fee was £500 and pretty much every other range manufacturer had said no. Bill - who did not have two pennies to rub together - said yes straight away. In spite of being the main sponsor, Bill's only influence over how the competition worked was a clause about Florigo being the main sponsor until he declined or the format changed, plus a rule that the criteria for winning the competition should be attainable by any ordinary operator.

At about the same time in 1987, Bill's dream of turning his concept into a force to be reckoned with took a giant leap forward when he was contacted by Jean Ritson. Shaw knew as soon as he met her that she was going to be a very special customer indeed. Jean Ritson had been in the fish and chip business for over a decade, starting at first in a shop called The Happy Haddock in Lancashire. She started Bizzie Lizzie's in 1986 in a small shop in Swadford Street in Skipton and she had decided to grow her operation on a new Canalside development, still in Skipton, just two years later.

She, like so many other friers, had been both intrigued and taken in by the net cast by Jean Shaw, and Bill saw the potential of her new site to be a mega-shop. Centrally located too! Bill held Jean Ritson's hand, not

 that she needed much assistance. Quite the opposite in fact, as she always knew exactly what she wanted. She may not have realised it at the time, but she was a major contributor to Bill's extremely steep learning curve, with Bizzie Lizzie's being the first new build from scratch. Bill had no other customers at the time.

Jean - centre above, and her team at Bizzie Lizzie's after winning Fish and Chip Shop of the Year in 1999

Jean Ritson and Bill Shaw both realised that they had the opportunity to create the perfect shop without compromise. He supplied all of her equipment (not just the frying range) and when she paid Bill up front for the whole job, it literally transformed his fortunes and generated some desperately needed cash flow. Bizzie Lizzie's was an awesome shop with a fantastic, forward-thinking fish frier at the helm in Jean Ritson. Bill delivered on spec and Jean allowed Bill to showcase the site to other operators from all four corners of the land – myself included. It was like dropping a boulder into the middle of a mill pond.

Bill's car could have driven itself to Bizzie Lizzie's over the next twelve months. Any forward thinking fish frier had to go and see it. The two Jeans worked closely together building the name – one in the public domain and the other in the trade. Holding open days in Skipton for operators (another great recruiting tool) Bill forged a friendship with Jean Ritson and her family that he still values and maintains today.

Bill bought out Ray Claridge in 1990 and continued to make steady progress. If you are in the business, then all of the following names will be familiar to you. If you are simply a lover of the dish then these names represent many of the biggest names in the trade. They all, at some stage, benefited from Bill Shaw's expertise in varying degrees, Arthur King (Jack's chain of shops), Tony McDermott (McDermotts), John Low (Ashvale Group), Philip Lye (Seafare chain of shops) Simon and Adrian Tweedale (Elite Group). There were literally dozens more. Clients were bombarded with innovative marketing, visuals, news and then, once a order was placed, a VIP factory trip to Holland at Bill's expense to see the manufacturing process and make the customer feel even more special. All of this backed up with the fact that the equipment itself was superbly built, easy to clean and capable of producing excellent fish and chips.

> *If Jean Ritson was the foothold Bill had been looking for, then my brother and I represented a notable scalp on the way up too*

If Jean Ritson was the foot-hold Bill had been looking for, then my brother and I represented a notable scalp on the way up too. We had no idea that we were even on his radar. As far as we were concerned, we made the enquiry and Bill was attending to our needs. Bill had however planted the seeds several months before with us at the Chip Barons' Ball because we matched perfectly the type of customer he needed to open up a brand new market.

In his list of top five shops that follow the end of his story, Petrou Brothers of Chatteris features. This was big news to me and quite extraordinary when you consider that this man has been responsible for more than two thirds of all of the 22 shops to win the National Fish and Chip Shop of the Year title. He has had over 100 finalists and his list of clients will probably make up more than 60% of any list of top shops worth visiting today. We feature in his top five because in his words "We have achieved so much with such an ordinary site." I don't really buy it myself, preferring to rely on the conversation we had last week, when he revealed that we were actually "The First Greeks to go Dutch!" and this is likely to be the real reason why our shop is held in such high regard by him.

We allowed Bill to display us like a trophy that he could show off to other Greeks, who were always likely to be a tough market for Bill to break into. Greeks had been, in the past, loyal users of a particular type of traditional frying range made by a company called Preston and Thomas. Bill knew that my brother and I were young and forward-thinking. He also knew that united, we would be able to persuade our father who had retired, that a change of direction was in order after buying seven P & T ranges in the past. He was right - and after transforming our shop in 1993, he had another superb site to which he could bring his prospective Greek customers that was actually being run by people with a Greek surname.

Bill sold the UK rights to sell Florigo ranges to ServEquip in 1993, a move that strengthened its ability to service the needs of its growing customer base. Bill stayed on at ServEquip until 1995 and when his contract ended with them, he simply walked away. He shifted his attention to becoming an operator and opened a couple of shops in the M1/A1 corridor called "Copperfields". The project gave him the opportunity to experience the dream he had been selling and to be fair he answered a few critics (like I said, Bill wasn't everyone's best friend) when he made the regional final of Fish and Chip Shop of the Year with one of his own sites. It left him wanting and unfulfilled, though, and once news had spread that Bill Shaw was no longer selling Florigo ranges, it wasn't long before he was approached to sell another brand of Dutch frying range.

With Florigo still very highly regarded in the capable hands of Robert Furey, Bill Shaw did it all over again with Kiremko KFE

With Florigo still very highly regarded by Bill and now prospering in the safe hands of Robert Furey, Bill Shaw did it all over again with Kiremko KFE and although he still engages in selling ranges at the time of writing this book, nothing he does in the future will compare to the monumental shift in direction he was able to convince a whole industry to embrace with nothing more than a 12 month contract and a smile.

Now with four grown up daughters all excelling in their chosen career paths, Bill and Jean are enjoying more than ever the fruits of their labour - they always did know how to party! Bill Shaw brought Dutch ranges into the mainstream, He taught fish friers how to market their businesses and how to raise their game. With the evolution of Dutch ranges and ultimately the arrival of HE pan technology, fish and chips by modern standards is now a healthy choice. Bill Shaw single-handedly dragged an industry bruised and dazed by the fast food revolution back into the fight and in the closing rounds, ground out a win on points...

No one else gets to have two top five lists in my book – but here are Bill Shaw's top five shops of all time and his top five shops around today.

Bill's Top Five ever: *Bizzie Lizzies, Chez Fred, McDermotts, Ashvale, Seafare.*
Bill's Top Five today: *Elite (Triton Road), Colman's, Petrou Brothers, Thornton Fisheries, Hanbury's.*

Fourth corner

Ask the best of the rest and most will agree. He is this generation of friers' choice for the best in the game – bar none. I had waited 20 years to hear his story and, boy, was it worth it. When I met him for the first time in 1995, it was after he had become a fish frying celebrity. He was the first person to do the job who actually looked under fifty and dressed like a chef. He was truly someone to look up to, at an age when both my brother and I really needed inspiration, focus and direction. I am completely convinced that this ever-so-unassuming and down to earth guy has had a truly amazing career and has made an incredible impact on so many fish friers. If he ever reads these words, perhaps he might begin to understand.

He described himself to me as quite lazy, but - to me - he should have been what Harry Ramsden ultimately failed to be and that is the undisputed King of Fish and Chips. Had he been just a decade later arriving on the planet, he would have truly cracked the whole job in every respect. If the development of high efficiency pans had arrived a decade sooner and a friendship forged out of business continued in a professional capacity, Ronald MacDonald would have certainly ended up back in the Circus. I'm honoured to be reproducing in his own words, his journey to date in what he considers to be any ordinary man's time in the trade.

Fred Capel - for who else could it be? - was born to Margaret and Peter Capel in May 1963 and had a typical childhood up to the age of 15. His father was a greengrocer in Hillingdon in West London in 1979 and was beginning to feel the heat from supermarkets. A genuine desire

Fred Capel

to come away from fruit and veg and city living gave Peter the idea for an idyllic little guest house by the seaside and after searching around, he found a 13 bedroom place in the Triangle in Bournemouth. Fred remembers that the career change almost killed his mother and in an attempt to help her (and the fact that he had left school without completing his final year) Fred found a six-week sandwich-making course at the renowned Bournemouth College in the Bournemouth

Echo newspaper. Fred learned of a further course at the college from a lecturer there who had spotted potential in him for more than sandwich-making. This was to accelerate his prospects immensely.

The two-year City and Guilds Hotel Chef Diploma offered him a 6 months work experience placement in one of London top hotels as part of the second year learning. Lacking the required O level entry grades, Fred had to earn his place on the course by impressing in an interview he had to plead for and by showing the determination and genuine enthusiasm which many have to come to admire since. Fred enrolled on the course and Peter and Margaret sold the guest house within nine months of buying it and took the lease on an old fashioned Tea Room in Burley in the New Forest.

The Inn on the Park on Hyde Park Corner was Hotel of the Year 1981 and Fred's appointment there for six months training saw him excel. He found himself completely at home as an apprentice and completed his 706.1 and 2 along with 707.1 and 2 (even though now replaced, it's the Chef qualification still sought after by employers today). At the end of the course, Fred was awarded "Larder Chef of the Year." He decided that he wanted the advanced cookery and larder qualification (706.3) as well and enrolled on a day release basis.

> *Fred had access to and, indeed, was working with the finest ingredients and top chefs of the time*

Finished at the Inn, he crossed the road and found full time employment at the Intercontinental – also on Hyde Park Corner. In both the classroom and his working environment, Fred had access to and, indeed, was working with the finest ingredients and top chefs of the time. Fred cites his inspiration at the time as the well-known Greek chef Nico Ladenis, whose Chez Nico in Mayfair boasted three Michelin stars.

Meanwhile Peter Capel had found a freehold tearoom for sale at Lyndhurst (New Forest again) and as is the norm, the pair went undercover for a cuppa to check it out along with a shop fitter called Leslie Atkins who was to give them advice on the price of refurbishing the site. It was at this meeting that the dream for Fred's dad Peter of actually owning his own tearoom was put to bed. The site required so much work that it was not viable to proceed.

During the conversation, however, Les said "Have you ever thought about fish and chips?" This unassuming question was born from the fact that Les had at the time been shop-fitting several sites for the "Superfish" company based in Ewell.

The very next day Fred and his folks went to a shop Les had recently completed and after doing some crude sums, Fred decided that fish and chips was "gonna be a walk in the park!" Leaving the city behind them,

Fred joined forces with his dad and they found a shop on Poole Road - the "second busiest road in Dorset." They called it "The Fisherman's Kitchen" and it was takeaway only. "At the time, fish and chips were 75p a portion – 50p for the fish and 25p for the chips. Week one when we opened, we did two and a half grand and couldn't cope," Fred said, "but within six months we were down to 900 quid a week." He remembers they were haemorrhaging cash, too.

"In a professional kitchen in those days, you turned up to a gleaming environment, turned it into a war zone and went home. The fairies (kitchen porters) would restore it to perfection before you arrived the next day. As a chef or even as a hotel kitchen back then, you never considered profit. That came from selling rooms for the night. I never gave it a second thought and I was totally unprepared for running a takeaway. I underestimated the job in such a big way!"

Fred and Peter spent three years there and when they left, it was turning over a healthy £4,500 a week, although it had at times both tested and galvanised their relationship – something that most father and son operators in our trade can, I'm sure, relate to. Ask Fred himself, as he is now training his own son Tom! Fred's dad had friends who were making good money from rest homes and Fred was beginning to crave financial independence from Peter and so he went back to the trusted Bournemouth Echo and found - ironically! - a lease available on a failing fruit and veg shop in Stour Road in Christchurch for just £3,500. The rent was only £6,000 a year and so they made an offer, subject to planning consent for A3 use. Fortunately, the shop already had consent and was worth considerably more than the asking price because of it.

Fred Capel and family: L to R: brother Nick, Brenda (Nan), Fred, Margaret and Peter (Mum and Dad) in 1990 at the first Chez Fred

Peter jokingly came up with the name "Chez Fred" (a tongue-in-cheek homage to Fred's hero) and at the time Fred wasn't impressed or convinced. He had £10,000 worth of equity in his modest home and a reasonable rapport with his Barclays Bank manageress because of his three year track record at the Fisherman's Kitchen. The economic climate at the time saw banks throwing money at pretty much anyone, according to Fred, and the £28,000 he borrowed was "easy to get, especially as she loved the name too. I decided to keep it, and on April Fools Day 1988, I opened the first Chez Fred."

All hands were on deck to help. Fred, his wife Carolyn, Peter and Margaret Capel all mucked in. There were 12 seats in his restaurant – three tables of four - and Fred instantly knew that sit-down was where he wanted to be. Week One and Chez Fred Mk I took £3,500.

Business was very good but Fred desperately wanted to own a freehold premises rather a leasehold site. He found a run-down chippy on Seamoor Road in Westbourne which had been a fish and chip shop in the 1940s, and had become one again when it had opened as "The Buccaneer" in 1968. It still had the original brown and orange Formica décor, was in desperate need of modernisation and was declaring takings of £2,500 a week. The freehold price was £275,000 and Fred wanted it straight away. His first Chez Fred was less than a year old and although doing very well, Fred knew he had to find a big chunk of money as a deposit to secure the funding he would need to acquire and refurbish the Buccaneer. He persuaded his father to buy the first Chez Fred from him for £125,000 and this gave Fred enough money to go back to his bank manageress at Barclays with a deposit and a plan.

Fred and Peter went 50/50 on the Buccaneer and pumped £425,000 into buying and refurbishing it. They repaid an old debt by employing the services of Leslie Atkins (the tea room advisor!) to undertake the shop fitting. More accomplished this time in the finer art of running a business, both father and son had calculated that they needed to take £7,500 per week to break even. They opened the new, improved and full sized Chez Fred on April 3rd 1989 - exactly one year and two days after the first Chez Fred had opened. It took an impressive £8,500 the first week and within four months was taking £17,000 every week. Although it was yet not quite the finished article, Fred entered his shop in the Seafish Fish and Chip Shop of the Year competition and at the very first attempt made it to the final, just losing out to the Ashvale in Scotland.

The following year Fred entered again and at only his second attempt, he made it again into a particularly tough final group of seven extremely good operators. Hanbury's, Squire's and Smiffy's were all huge names in the trade in those days, but it was not to be their year. Fred remembers - with a rare display of anything other than reserved composure - the huge cheer that went up around the room and the feeling of utter relief, acceptance and elation. It was like nothing he had ever experienced before or since. In November 1991 Chez Fred became the best fish and chip shop in the UK and, in my opinion, has been ever since. In Chapter Five, I will explain more about what makes this shop so special but for now, I am really keen to continue with Fred's story - after all, it is Fred himself that is one of my four corners in this chapter.

In November 1991, Chez Fred became the best fish and chip shop in the UK and, in my opinion, has been ever since

The exposure from winning earned Fred a lot of attention but he never believed his own publicity. "However good we are this year, we have to be better next year," he said. For the next couple of years, Fred turned his golden batter into golden profit. Riding the crest of the wave and eager to capitalise on his successful and winning formula, Fred began to explore the potential of franchising and when an opportunity came to roll out his brand he admits he was almost blinded by the idea rather than the physical mechanics and logistical challenges of actually dividing his time between sites.

What started out as the next logical step in Fred's mind turned out to be probably the darkest period of his career. With four other partners, Chez Fred No 3 opened as a test site for franchising in Golders Green - a strong Jewish community in North London. At the end of 1993 and the beginning of 1994 the new shop had great turnover (£10,000+ a week)

but was failing to make money. The only positive he recalls from that time was a relationship he formed with a man called Ian Neill – who grew to become Fred's mentor and one of his closest friends. Ian realised that Fred wasn't ready for franchising due to the huge compromises required in rolling out a brand to multiple sites from a hands-on single site operation.

High rent, labour costs and disputes between the partners brought the experiment to a swift and unsatisfactory conclusion. Fred walked away from the whole experience emotionally and financially bruised. Ian helped Fred to exit the deal in the middle of 1994 with his brand still intact and he went back to Bournemouth to continue work at his award-winning store, which was still very much at the sharp end of the industry and blazing trails.

One year later and Ian came to Fred with a completely new proposition. Already hugely successful at developing franchise brands (being general manager of Pizza Express) Neill wanted Fred take a share in another pilot shop and input his operational expertise. Their concept – Whitecaps - came at a time when Fred was distracted and he now regrets not having put enough effort into it. As a visitor myself, I was blown away by the forward-thinking concept and feel now that they were far ahead of the frying technology of the time, which was nowhere near advanced enough to deliver the consistency in product that they needed. Had they been able to de-skill the operation enough and meet the needs of a successful roll out franchise formula it would have prospered tremendously.

An opportunity for Ian came to take another unknown brand called Wagamama and develop it further and Fred and Ian decided to sell Whitecaps and go their separate ways on very amicable terms. Ian Neill is now Chairman of Wagamama and is widely regarded as The Authority in relaxed dining offers within the restaurant world.

The next fifteen years bringing us up to the present time - just like the first fifteen years of Fred's story - require far less detail. He extended his shop in 1999 and increased the size of his restaurant to finally achieve the 60/40 restaurant/take away dynamic he had always wanted. His father retired in 2000 and in 2010, Fred's son Tom now shows the flair and promise that Fred himself exhibited in 1981.

> *He has travelled further down the road to perfection than any other - before or since*

But whilst short on detail, it's these last fifteen years that have really defined Fred Capel for me as the most significant fish and chip operator of our time. He has travelled further down the road towards perfection than any other - before or since - and I am convinced that the Chez Fred brand would have achieved world domination had he just been able to deliver it to his own exacting standards!

Fred Capel has been continuously pushing the standards of our trade higher and higher at his site in Westbourne. If there's something you like about your local chippy, Fred will have either considered it before them, shared it with them or inspired them through someone else they saw do it who had copied him. He really has looked harder at every aspect of the business than anyone else I've ever met.

Everything happens in his shop for a reason and the reason is normally the best one. At face value, you may think that his journey is typical of many in the trade but you would be wrong. I was born to be a fish frier and although I always wanted to be like Fred Capel, it's never the same to follow in someone else's footsteps as it is walking a path for the first time. Fred Capel should never have been a fish frier. He chose to be one. He broke the mould in every way. He took the industry by storm, challenged every practice along the way and improved not one big thing but literally hundreds of little things.

His timing was wrong because he came along before the industry - and the technology that served it - was ready to allow him to achieve

Fred with Fish and Chip Shop of the Year 2009/10 finalists John McNeill of Scooby Snax (left) and Daniel Pettitt of Daniel's

his full potential and Fred made the decision not to bother rather than achieve anything other than perfection.

> *Fred was the man who could have taken America by storm and made fish and chips a global phenomenon. He still is that man...*

Fred was the man who could have taken America, or any deprived market for that matter, by storm, and made fish and chips a global phenomenon. He still is that man, because he has chosen to remain at the top of his game all this time and could now take advantage of all the components that were missing when he explored the then-flawed concept decades ago. He very much admires Andrew Constantinou, who - now that the enabling technology and practices are firmly in place - is rolling out a chain of shops that are setting the standards today for multiple operators.

Fred Capel refuses to stop learning and continues to share and when you visit his shop the attention to detail is so very, very good and so very, very slick and so polished you don't even notice how fabulous it is until it's over and you wish you had the ability to experience it again.

I fear that at this time in his life, timing will be the ultimate factor that denies both fish and chips and the rest of the world the benefit of his full potential, as he just doesn't need to be all that he could be any more. Today, Fred Capel could easily reproduce his brand for the masses all over the world. At 47 however, Fred has achieved a material wealth and level of comfort that makes him happy and as happy as that makes me feel for him, I still can't help feeling sorry for everyone else.

Chapter Five – my pick of the top five shops to visit in the UK and why

I cannot put them into any order – so don't even ask me to try. These five shops are all so special, all so unique and all so damn good in their own right that to me they are almost beyond comparison. I have visited more chip shops than you've had hot dinners – guaranteed. I've seen the really, really bad ones – where you wipe your feet on the way out and I've picked these five shops as my crème de la crème. I've done so for so many different reasons that I am going to have to explain each one on an individual basis. I tried to use a formula to report them all to you on in a uniform manner. This proved to be extremely difficult as they are all so individual in their concept, operation and delivery of essentially what is supposed to be the same end result. One for example is technically faultless and another gives the ultimate customer experience. The masters of each particular establishment are also so richly diverse in fortune and origin and yet all so similar in purpose and sentiment. At the end of the chapter, I'm gonna give you another list of another dozen or so extremely-worth-a-visit shops. Many of these shops have never won awards and without a book like this to put them on the radar, they would simply remain local treasures in their own communities and that just wont do at all! So read on and join the fast track to fish and chip paradise……..

Colman's of South Shields

"Quality isn't expensive – it's priceless"… As soon as the words have left his mouth, you know you are dealing with a man who has real passion for his life's work. Richard Ord has more reason than most to care as much as he does, too. He's carrying the legacy of four generations at his site on the famous Ocean Road in South Shields. In 1905 his great grandmother opened a refreshment "hut" on the beach foreshore.

She was an Italian immigrant with the surname Turrichi, which she felt did nothing to promote her business and so she gave it the authentic English name of Frankie's. Business was brisk. Within five years she had constructed a proper sit down restaurant on the beach and by 1926 the site in Ocean Road had been acquired and a marriage had taken place to a Mr Colman.

Colman's daughter ran the shop after them and was in her turn followed by another daughter, who eventually provided the business with a son. Richard Ord, born in June 1954, lived above the shop as a child and blames a lifetime of memories for inspiring him every day to achieve the very high standards that he does. He still remembers fondly his mother going to the quay side every day to collect fish. He remembers, too, the 112lb sacks of potatoes that were back breaking to move around (especially at the age of 12 when he started working there to help out) and he also remembers the local branch of the NFFF holding regular meetings in the function room upstairs in the 1950's and 60's.

He learned his trade on a traditional English style frying range and always knew that he would ultimately end up in charge. That happened in 1990 – the year Richard married Frances - and he commented on how he visited Harry Ramsden's Original store in Guisley around that time and saw many ways to improve his own business based on their performance. A slow program of modernisation began, although Richard was always mindful to retain the sense of history and charm attached to the building, whilst pushing his boundaries higher on choice, quality and value. Richard pretty much did his own thing for many years, earning Colman's a reputation locally that was second to none.

He liked to spend some of his free time studying other people's operations and going to trade exhibitions and after making the acquaintance of Bill Shaw, he began to consider the benefits of changing his operation to accommodate high efficiency pan technology. This became a fait accompli in 2003.

At this time, Richard wasn't really concerned with creating a profile for himself within the frying community. But then he met Duncan

McLean – Marketing Director of Henry Colbeck Ltd, a leading supplier to the frying trade. Duncan is an extremely capable, well-respected and professional expert in the promotion and marketing of fish and chips. He invited Richard to accompany him to the Fish and Chip Shop of the Year 2006 finals in January 2007 and it was after seeing possibly the most handsome frier ever to have walked the earth lift the National title (that would be me, I think...) that Richard considered entering his own shop.

By this time, Richard Ord's shop was a very organised, yet warm, experience for patrons. His product was first class and his team of staff very helpful and friendly. Fred Capel ranks Richard's shop in his top five favourite shops, remarking that Colman's special hand prepared scampi was better than any he had tasted anywhere before or since. With the influence of both Bill and Duncan infused into Richard's well oiled operation, Colman's started to collect awards like they were on special offer.

The first gong worth noting was the 2007 BBC Food and Farming award, followed very quickly by the UKTV Food Hero national winner in the same year. The £40,000 prize money bought Richard a second – and much needed - frying range to help him cope with the rising trade levels his success was bringing him. Colman's made the finals in the Fish and Chip Shop of the Year competition in both 2007 and 2008 and in 2009 became the first shop to lift the brand new "Good Catch Award" recognising sustainable practices.

His mission is to dispel the myth and get the healthy message out there

Colman's fry in palm oil – not the norm for that neck of the woods, it has to be said - but it allows the excellent flavour of the fish to really break through. The shop employs a full time filleter to prepare the fish for frying and speciality fish still comes in fresh daily from the quay side at Sunderland. Cod is sourced responsibly from Icelandic waters, and Richard opts for line-caught, tightly graded 8-10 ounce frozen at sea fillets. The batter is a secret recipe

- delicate and crisp and just the right side of golden - and although Richard prefers not to have an alcohol license, he encourages customers to bring their own tipple and this is supported by the customers that like a glass of naughty with their meal. Freshly squeezed orange juice is on tap, kids' activities are plentiful and there are lots of really nice touches wherever your eyes wander around the restaurant.

For example the photo galleries, the place settings - made to look like a freshly folded newspaper full of Colman's information - and even the branded cutlery and crockery provoke an unexpected smile. Richard and his lovely wife and team richly deserve their success. He hates the way fish and chips is used as a stereotype for bad food because he knows how good a meal it really is. His mission is to dispel the myth and "get the healthy message out there."

I have asked literally hundreds of friers during my research to name their favourite five shops. It's little wonder that Colman's of South Shields featured in more top fives than any other shop at this time in the UK. It belongs on any real fish and chip fanatics "must do" list because it is a shop of the moment and yet at the same time it has such a fantastic sense of history and tradition. When you visit Colman's, you get wrapped up in layer upon layer of really genuine warm northern hospitality. You also get a really excellent meal every time and great value for money too.

Richard's Top Five: *Chez Fred - Bournemouth, The Magpie - Whitby, Petrou Brothers - Chatteris, Mermaids Tail – Leicester Sq, Kailif – Freemantle, Perth*

COLMAN'S OF SOUTH SHIELDS

182 - 186 Ocean Road, South Shields, Tyne and Wear, England, NE33 2JQ

Tel: 0191 456 1202

Opening times:

Restaurant - 11.00am until 5.45pm

Takeaway - 11.00am until 6.45pm

Fish available: cod, line-caught haddock, plaice, lemon sole, gurnard, turbot, pollack, whiting, hake, an assortment of fishcakes, scampi, calamari, scallops, crab, lobster and mussels.

Bizzie Lizzie's of Skipton

> *When I look into the display, I can see if what we're selling looks happy or not. If it's not happy, we throw it out and start again!*

Jean Ritson is a lady. Her date of birth and any other vital statistics of personal interest to you will have to be revealed by alternative means. I am far too well adjusted to ask and therefore I have decided that it is of no benefit to anyone reading this book. It doesn't matter how old she is, anyway, nor how she came to be at The "Happy" Haddock in Barnoldswick, Lancashire, then at Northcliffe Fisheries in Shipley and also Park Fisheries in Cleckheaton before establishing Bizzie Lizzie's in Swadford Street, Skipton in 1986. The important point to note is this…stop the presses for breaking news…women can fry fish too!

Jean Ritson is a very special lady indeed. A mould breaker, a true pioneer and a visionary. Bizzie Lizzie's in Skipton was evolutionary. The first of its kind, it heralded the start of an exciting new chapter in the history of our trade. Her unique perspective makes her still today without comparison. Interviewing her for this book was inspiring for me. Having met her on a few occasions over the years, I already knew her to be genuine, warm and sincere. Get her to open up about her favourite subject and she articulates in a language all of her own – but it needs no translation. "Every thing has to be happy," she says. "The batter has to be happy, the potatoes have to be happy and the fish has to be happy." She added "When I look into the display, I can see if what we're selling looks happy or not. If it's not happy, we throw it out and start again!" Jean Ritson will not fail on one thing. She settles for nothing less than absolute perfection. In conversation, she demonstrates clearly the level of her attention to detail, refusing to compromise on even the smallest thing. "I like to look after outside. There has to be a welcoming light, staff must smile, they must be impeccably presented and good housekeeping has to have taken place. I have a never-quite-good enough attitude and when it comes to chips, I much prefer to give than to receive. Chips are only perfect if I have a second one."

Remembering her early relationship with Bill Shaw and how she enabled him to begin his incredible journey, Jean makes some very honest observations. Jean felt inspired by the whole Florigo concept. She wanted different, she wanted modern and was fed up with many of

*Bizzie Lizzie's celebrate their 2010
Five Star Friers Quality Award*

her comrades who often lied about what they did because they felt ashamed by their chosen profession. She couldn't understand why so many had become so negative and sloppy. Jean was incredibly proud of what she did and wanted to give the trade a "kick up the behind" in an attempt to make fish and chips be all that it could be.

Already very experienced at frying, when the opportunity to expand her operation at the canal site in Skipton presented itself, Jean knew that she wanted to be different to every other operator. She openly admits, though, "I had a clear vision in my head of what I wanted to achieve but remember at the time, I didn't even know what a logo was." Her vision was realised by Bill Shaw who helped Jean Ritson achieve the marketing concept by marrying his skills to her passion. Jean was very much the driving force to this working relationship though and it's summed up in one sentence "I can live with my own mistakes but not anyone else's." Not that she's ever made any because her strength has always been "longevity for fun." When you visit Bizzie Lizzie's, takeaway or restaurant, it feels like coming home on a winter's night. You are greeted with warmth in the welcome and the décor and the ambience. Pleasing to the eye, the restaurant is comfortable and light and the service prompt but never rushed. The meal is always superb and served by a surrogate Aunt or Uncle. When you consider that it has been like this for almost a quarter of a century – it's no wonder the roll of honour attached to this shop is longer than Her Majesty's New Years Honours list.

Not being a bloke has given Jean Ritson a different perspective to just about any other operator before or since. Sure there have been some talented female friers since – Susan Yeung (now Ord), Lindsey Petrie (now Richardson) are two great examples - but Jean Ritson was not only the first to install a Dutch range in the UK, she was also the mother of inspiration to a whole new generation of master friers and her shop is as inspiring today as it was nearly a quarter of a century ago. Today Jean Ritson still has an eye for detail. She can hear down the phone if her shop is happy and she cleans when nothing is dirty. Everything about her shop is amazing and so is everything about her.

Jean's Top Five: *Trenchers - Whitby, Wetherby Whalers, Wepsters - Baildon, the Seafare chain and Chez Fred*

BIZZIE LIZZIE'S
36 Swadford Street, Skipton, North Yorkshire, BD23 1QY
Tel: 01756 793189 / 01756 701131 (restaurant)
Opening times:
Monday   11:00am - 11:15pm
Tues - Thur 11:00am - 11:30pm
Friday   11:00am - Midnight
Saturday   11:00am - Midnight
Sunday   11:00am - 11:15pm
Fish available: cod, haddock, fishcake (scallop), plaice and scampi

Pete's Chippery of Bedworth

There is only ever one winner. No one remembers the guy who finished second. Well, this chip shop needs to be recognised. It needs to be on your list of shops to visit for several reasons.

Firstly – it is technically the best I've ever seen. In terms of layout, space, practicality and workability – it ticks every box and then some.

Secondly – if it were in any other part of the country or up against any lesser competition, it would surely have won Fish and Chip Shop of the Year.

Thirdly – the guy who was running this shop for his family is so good at what he does, he has earned the respect of just about anyone who has really got to know him.

Petrakis (Pete) Theocharous was the youngest of four kids (two sisters and a brother) and born in Derby in 1957. His father Stelios had come to England several years earlier in search of his fortune and opened a café-diner. Growing up, Pete learned to understand Greek, but English was his first language. He helped his father in his business and opened his first chip shop under a bridge behind Narborough Road in Leicester in the early seventies. He closed it down due to its awful position and went to work with his uncle at "Marios Chippery" where he saved for several years in the hope of one day owning his own shop. Pete married Angela in June 1979 and they didn't want to waste time before starting a family.

Within a year, Pete found a shop in Croft Road, Nuneaton and decided it was the perfect place to raise his young and "Pete's Chippery" was born.

That man put in some hours. He worked long and hard, determined to provide for his family. His aim was to build a business and a home and he devoted his life for the next twenty years to doing just that. His daughters Vas and Hambou arrived first, followed by his first son Stelios in 1984 and then his second son George in 1986. By the time the brothers were 22 and 20 respectively, Pete had been on his feet for the best part of 26 years. In that time, he had earned a reputation locally for producing excellent fish and chips and being a principled man of good report. The boys, too, were well known and had spent their whole lives in the fish and chip shop environment. Both had been mentored by their father and were full of enthusiasm and energy for the job.

Another fish and chip shop in nearby Bedworth, a former award-winning site, came up for sale and Pete considered it for his sons but missed out on it. He refitted the shop in Croft Road with a Kiremko high efficiency Dutch range from Bill Shaw and during that time the new owners of the shop in Bedworth that Pete had had his eye on were struggling. It went rapidly downhill, and in 2006, Pete acquired it after it had closed down and fallen into disrepair. I met Stelios for the first time by chance at the 2005 Fish and Chip Shop of the Year finals when he collected an award for Pete's Chippery's charity work and I was canvassing support for chippychat.co.uk.

The shop I would build if I had a blank canvas and a blank cheque.

We were both unaware of the future that lay ahead for both of us. I went on to win Fish and Chip Shop of the Year the following year and Stelios, George and their father invested heavily in the development of the Bedworth site for the new Pete's Chippery.

They chucked literally thousands of pounds and every spare minute they had at it. There were no professional designers, though. Every element of the whole project was developed by the trio; all the way down to the very smallest detail. The learning curve must have been steep and the mix of both experience and enthusiasm resulted in a shop that screams both common sense and flair wherever you look. Removing the first floor in the front of the premises creates a vaulted ceiling and

a waiting area for the customer that impresses, adds to the experience and creates the perfect space to present the food offer. The centerpiece is of course the custom built Florigo island range. This one is unique and has a complete back bar section with an integral canopy suited into place. A parade of tills and a custom built refrigerated display make up the front counter and help to keep queues nice and short. Where the customer doesn't get to see is the absolute best work space I've seen anywhere - ever. Everything makes sense and has the best quality anything

Top L to R: Stelios, Pete and George
Below: Stelios at the custom range

you can get. Even the staff toilet flushes with a sensor so that there is no risk of cross contamination. Pete's Chippery in Bedworth is a true masterpiece.

The food is good too, so good in fact that Stelios - who opened the shop and earned the Seafish Frier's Quality award there - has since put his own batter recipe into production and is enjoying very good sales of it across the country. The shop narrowly lost the place in the finals of Fish and Chip Shop of the Year 2007 to Andy's of Swadlincote (who had been finalists three years in a row) and would have been certain favourites to win, but it was not meant to be.

The shop has its own car-park and I know that Pete and his sons are planning to expand the Bedworth site to include sit-down in the very near future. George is the leading man in the business these days and he is the only man I know who can turn a BMW into a time machine – often arriving before he sets off, he has absolutely no comprehension of fear whatsoever. Their branding is excellent, the seasonal species of fish they offer is exciting and all other menu items are prepared to very high standards too. A lovely family, a lovely family story and a shop that really impresses, I recommend a visit for any operator or fish and chip fanatic to see the shop that I would build if I had a blank canvas and a blank cheque.

Stelios' Top Shops: *The Cottage – Blackpool, Ypas Chippy – Barnsley, Brownsover – Rugby*

PETE'S CHIPPERY
131 Nuneaton Road, Collycroft, Bedworth, CV12 8AP
Tel: 02476 733750
Opening times: Monday – Saturday 12.00 – 2.00   4.00 – 10.00
Fish available: cod, haddock, seasonal specials.

Ypas Chippy of Kexborough

In 1968, Ken and Gina (Regina were 'er Sunday name but she'll not thank me fo' telling thee that) Watson were already married and had a one year old son called Brent. Ken at this time was helping Gina's dad - who had been a successful cook in the Army - in his fish and chip shop. Fast forward twenty odd years and that shop was long gone, Brent was grown up and spraying cars but not really making a living and Ken got made redundant from the local coal mine to which his career had eventually steered him.

Ken had been a successful cook in the Army and at this time was helping Gina's dad in his fish and chip shop

By now, you've figured out these folks are from up north. At around the time the country was properly on its knees, Ken found an empty shop in Monk Bretton near Barnsley and invited his son to join him in selling motorbike spares to make a living.

Ken being the practical fellow that he is decided to check with the local council that his intended plan for the site was acceptable to them. When they informed him that it was in fact a former fish and chip shop, his plan changed. He opened a chippy using his redundancy money and then swapped that site for a smaller shop but a better location in Kexborough.

A very brief history I know – but it's important all the same because I need you to understand how ordinary (in a "just like us" kind of way) this family was. Everything that has happened to them including the rest of their story might be typical of any one reading this book – but it's not, because they are actually really, really special.

Swapping the first chippy for a smaller one might sound crazy but Ken knew straight away that it was a good deal because of where it was. Being smart enough to adapt his plans when he discovered the first

Ken and Gina Watson

*Ypas - then (inset) and now, ten years later...and the shop is currently
undergoing another refit, step by step as time and funds allow*

empty shop was a former chippy was not only inspired, but it was our
good fortune as well because those two business decisions allowed the
Ypas chippy to open in 1991.

Built in around 1640 (that's right – 1640!) 135 Churchfield Lane,
Kexborough will almost certainly not be an address that means anything
to you. If however, you are a fish and chip fanatic, it will do from now
on – because if you don't visit this shop, then you might not have
experienced the best fish and chips money can buy. Originally this lock
up workshop was known as a fish and chip shop called "Howards" but
for how long, no one knows. After "Howards", Harry Hardcastle opened
it in 1933 and ran it until 1971 (that's an incredible amount of time to
stand up for – think about that for a moment - 38 years from dawn til
dusk!) After several quick changes of owner over the next 20 years, Ken
got it with the two pan range still in place and armed with the recipes
and training from May Shaw – his mother-in-law with whom he had
learned in 1968 - he began working the site.

It is an appropriate place in the story to describe the shop as it was
then. Basically, the Ypas Chippy (as in "why pass?") was a single storey
lockup cabin/hut. Compact and - because of its age - without a straight
wall, floor or ceiling in sight.

Ken was the sort of character who would have a go at just about
anything and his like-minded son Brent wanted to help his dad and

together they took on the challenge of trying to grow the business both in turnover and - if necessary - brick by brick.

Ken had kept racing pigeons for most of his life, and fell ill with an unfortunate illness because of his close proximity to them, just two months after opening. Brent, along with his wife Anne, suddenly found themselves at the helm with the responsibility of making the shop pay firmly at their feet. And there's little more to say after that – save for the new three pan Hopkins range they fitted in 1997. They won a competition in 1998 to find the best local chippy in the Barnsley Chronicle and over the years - as and when their savings would allow - have extended and built and improved and scrubbed and made the shop up to the standard you will find when you visit. They have achieved a maximum five stars in their local environmental health Scores on the Doors scheme as well as the Seafish Quality Award – which is the highest industry standard any shop can achieve.

When you go there as a customer, though, you won't see the hard work this couple have put in with their one (maybe two) members of staff. The shop is a still a humble little cabin but, trust me, it has absolutely everything you would hope to find in chip shop heaven. If it's open, then either Ann or Brent is always there.

Every piece of fish is cut to perfection and weighed on digital scales. Without skin or bone, you can choose cod, cod, cod or cod. They may as well have named every chip because they are so particular about giving the best chips that they use a very traditional make of chipper called an F2F – which is as old as the shop (probably), really unreliable but produces virtually no bits. Brent even has a spare (which some museum is desperate to own) to ensure that he doesn't have to settle for anything less than perfection. Their home-made fishcakes are the best I've ever tasted (better than mine!) and their batter and mushy peas are produced fresh on site every session to exacting recipes.

FISH & CHIPS - A NATIONAL TREASURE

Their homemade fishcakes are the best I have ever tasted (better than mine!)

As an operator myself, one can see when a fellow operator is in love with his job. Anne and Brent are the lungs and heart of Ypas Chippy. They breathe life into the site like no other two people could. They know every inch of their tiny little shop intimately and produce food and service that in my opinion puts most other operators (including myself) to shame. There are no frills and no gimmicks. They do what they do honestly and with pride.

I discovered them through my website www.chippychat.co.uk and made the journey to their shop to see it for myself after being told to do so by every other fellow frier that went before me. There is no bigger endorsement than that of professionals who know great fish and chips when they eat them. It's not about the size – it's all about the owners and the food they sell. I'm not saying they're the best. I am saying you really must go and see for yourself.

Brent and Anne prefer to not disclose their favourite five shops.

YPAS CHIPPY
135 Churchfield Lane Kexborough Barnsley Yorkshire
Tel: 01226 382 681
Opening times
Mon - 11.30 – 1.30
Tues, Wed, Thurs, Fri - 11.30 –1.30 4.30 – 7.30
Sat - 11.30 –2.00
Fish available: cod, fishcake, scampi

Chez Fred of Bournemouth

What makes a trip to Chez Fred so special? Whether you are a fish and chip fanatic, a hungry shopper or a very, very fortunate passer-by, your first visit to Chez Fred will always exceed your expectations. It doesn't matter if you've heard about the reputation, it doesn't matter if money is no object and it doesn't matter if you've searched all four corners of the country to sample the best fish and chips in the land – until you've been to Chez Fred you have only been kidding yourself.

It is terribly easy to explain. Everything that is functional is modest, pleasing and there for a reason. Every part of the experience is comfortable, enjoyable and memorable and everything that needs to be good is either superb or excellent. The décor is exactly what you would want a very good fish and chip shop restaurant to be like. The staff are friendly but not too familiar, professional and helpful. The food is of the highest standard and the price always less than you would have been more than happy to pay.

The decisions that are made before you even enter would astound you. The attention to detail is unlike anything I have experienced in any other single-site operation. It feels as polished as a brass button. The menu, the website, the sprat pack, the moggy bag, the branded kids treats all feel "corporate chain" but in a really good way. The food offer itself presents something for everyone and yet is not too big. Fresh ingredients – always sourced responsibly and locally when possible. The range of fresh fish delivered in five days a week is impressive – farmed halibut, whole plaice (on the bone), red gurnard, whiting, hake and haddock make the list but

Fred lecturing at the Fish and Chip Masterclass hosted by Marston Ales to mark the 150th Anniversary of fish and chips in April 2010

once they're gone, a simple line through the name on the specials board tells you what is still available. Cod at Chez Fred comes usually from the Faroe Islands where stocks are monitored and sustainable fishing takes place. It is frozen at sea within 4 hours of being caught, graded into fillets between 16 and 32 ounces - because Fred has found that size to be the best - and when they are defrosted and fried, they truly can be described as being fresher than fresh.

Fred fries his fish in groundnut oil – he likes to do this because he believes this frying medium imparts less flavour than other frying mediums, allowing his customers to really savour the taste of his produce. In contrast, he fries his chips in a different vegetable oil called rapeseed oil. He prefers the taste that this infuses into the potato during frying. The practice of using different mediums is one undertaken only by operators like Fred Capel who are in pursuit of absolute perfection. I can count the number of people I've met that do this on my noses.

> *Chez Fred is not just ahead of the game - it has been writing the rules of the game for the last twenty years*

When I talk about Fred's fish and chips, I must also point out that Fred will only buy the very best quality available. He can tell a customer on any given visit what boat, what grower and even what batch number any of his raw materials came from – not that anyone has ever asked. When quizzed about the wine on offer, Fred was eager to point out that when vinegar or lemon juice is on the palate or lips, the taste of wine can be distorted or destroyed and so both the new world and historical selections are chosen to accommodate and complement both the dish and its respective condiments perfectly.

Chez Fred is not just ahead of the game. It has been writing the rules of the game for the last twenty years. It is the benchmark that all other shops have to measure up to, because there has to be one that is the best.

Since it opened, it has become an overnight success, established itself as the best in the business and has never once looked like anything else. In my thirty eight years of breathing, I have only ever come across two other shops that came close and they are included in my top five. (One of those is also included in Fred's top five.)

To be at the very top for so so long is incredible and it looks like nothing is likely to change in a hurry. Fred Capel is never complacent and I know that in 2010 he is really fired up and has even more improvements in the pipeline. As a visitor, you will simply continue to have your expectations exceeded. What makes Chez Fred the ultimate fish and chip restaurant for me will probably never be appreciated by the customer.

That is why it is so damn good.

Fred's Top Five: *Seashell in Marylebone, Colman's of South Shields, The Magpie in Whitby, Hanbury's in Torquay, Squires in Barnstaple*

CHEZ FRED
10 Seamoor Road, Westbourne, Bournemouth
Tel: 01202 761023
Opening times:
Mon-Fri – 11:30am-2:00pm, 5:00pm-10:00pm
Saturday – 11:30am-2:30pm, 5:00pm-10:00pm
Sunday – 5:00pm-9:30pm
Fish available: cod, haddock, plaice, home-made salmon and cod fishcake, scampi, skate, rock, halibut and an assortment of specials served in the restaurant.

And you really need to visit these as well....

THE COVE
17 Bridge Street, Otley, Leeds LS21 1BQ.
Tel: 01943 462 120
Opening times:
Mon, Tues, Wed   11.30 -1.30   4.30 -7.30
Thurs, Fri, Sat   11.30 – 7.30
Sun   12.00 – 7.30
Fish available: haddock, plaice, tuna, halibut, sword fish, scampi.

BROWNSOVER
124 Hollowell Way, Rugby, Warwickshire CV21 1LT
Tel: 01788 571188
Opening times:
Mon-Sat - 11:30am-10:30pm
Fish available: cod, haddock and plaice

MCDERMOTTS
5, 6 & 7 Forestdale Shopping Centre, Featherbed Lane,
Croydon CR0 9AS
Tel: 020 8651 1440
Opening times:
Tuesday to Friday for lunch - 12.00pm to 2.00pm
Tuesday to Friday for dinner - 5.00pm to 9.30pm
Saturdays for lunch - 12.00pm to 2.00pm
Saturdays for dinner - 5.00pm to 9.00pm
Fish available: cod (skinned & boned) or haddock (skinned & boned), plaice fillet, rock salmon/huss, scampi in breadcrumbs - all fried in groundnut oil

ANSTRUTHER FISH BAR
42-44 Shore Street, Anstruther, Fife, KY10 3AQ
Tel: 01333 310518
Opening times:
11.30 - 22.00hrs takeaway, 11.30 - 21.30hrs restaurant, 7 days a week
Fish available: haddock, Icelandic cod, organic cod, mackerel, smoked haddock, prawns, lobster and crab, hake, pollock

THE BAY
The Beach Promenade, Stonehaven, Kincardineshire AB39 2RD
Tel: 01569 762000
Opening times:
12:00 noon until 10:00 pm, 7 days a week
Fish available: haddock, hake, pollock, coley, home-made fishcakes, fresh scampi, and a specials board which serves a variety of locally sourced fresh fish such as lemon sole, witches sole, tuna, langoustines and many more, most of which can be grilled or fried according to the customer's wishes.

THORNTONS FISHERIES
11, Victoria Rd East, Thornton-Cleveleys, Lancashire FY5 5HT
Tel: 01253 858668
Opening times:
Mon-Thurs - 11:30am-1:30pm, 4:30-7:00pm
Fri day - 11:30am-1:30pm, 4:30-8:00pm
Sat - 11:30am-1:30pm, 4:30-7:00pm
Fish available: haddock in 3 sizes, silver hake, halibut, plaice, alaskan pollock and a variety of specials depending on what is readily available.

THE FISH HOUSE
St Thomas Road, Brentwood, Essex CM14 4DB
Tel: 01277 221 772
Opening times:
Mon – Sat - 11.00 – 8.30
Fish available: cod, haddock, plaice, skate, rock, scampi, cod roe, lemon sole, pollock, seabass

HANBURYS
Princes Street, Babbacombe, Torquay, Devon, TQ1 3LW
Tel: 01803 329928
Opening times:

Mon - Sat	Lunch	Evening
Take Away	12 - 2	5 - 9
Restaurant	12 - 2	5:30 - 9

Fish available: cod, haddock, smoked haddock, plaice, lemon sole, monk fish, John Dory, hake, huss, skate

OLLEYS
65 – 67 Norwood Road, Herne Hill, London, SE24 9AA
Tel: 0208 671 8259, 0208 671 5665
Opening times
Mondayclosed   closed
Tuesday 12 – 3   5 – 10:30
Wednesday   12 – 3   5 – 10:30
Thursday   12 – 3   5 – 10:30
Friday   12 – 3   5 – 10:30
Saturday   12 – 3   5 – 10:30
Sunday   12 – 3   5 – 9:30
Fish available: cod, haddock, plaice, lemon sole, salmon, hake, escolar, sword, tuna, halibut, mahi mahi all either, fried, grilled/steamed or served in a tomato and herb sauce.

FRENCH'S
10 Quayside, Wells-next-the-Sea, Norfolk, NR23 1AH
Tel: 01328 710396
Opening times:
Winter:
Monday – closed
Tuesday – 11:45am-2:30pm, 4:30pm-7:30pm
Wednesday - 11:45am-2:30pm, 4:30pm-7:30pm
Thursday - 11:45am-2:30pm, 4:30pm-7:30pm
Friday - 11:45am-2:30pm, 4:30pm-9:00pm
Saturday – 11:45am-9:00pm
Sunday – 11:45am-7:00pm
Summer:
11:45am-10:30pm, 7 days a week
Fish available: cod, haddock, plaice, huss, skate, scampi

Chapter Six – mark my words...

Writing a column for Fish & Chips and Fast Food magazine began for me as an opportunity to communicate my ideas to other operators in the capacity of Top Chip Champ – when I won the National Fish and Chip shop of the year title. Four years on and I am still doing the job. Initially I used my platform to share ideas and promote positive approaches to success in the frying trade. Once the title had been passed onto the next ambassador, I felt far more comfortable in taking a more balanced view of the climate fish friers find themselves having to operate in. Here for your consideration are in my opinion some of the most honest observations I have been able to share about being a fish and chip shop operator in 2009/10.

APRIL 2009 • IT CAN HAPPEN TO ANYONE

This column I thought I would share with my readers a very honest story about a fish and chip shop owner who has had a very challenging year indeed. Let me know by writing in to fish and chips and fast food magazine if you have any similar stories to tell. You don't have to give your name and I'm afraid there won't be any prizes...

This chap does most things right...

This chap does most things right. His shop is a freehold, bought and paid for except for the new range he had fitted in 2005. He has served his local community for over 25 years, employed local people and supported local initiatives. He took over from his father in 1988 and has a reputation for miles and miles around for great fish and chips. Within the frying community too he is fairly well known and considered to be the sort of operator that other friers probably wouldn't mind being a penny behind. His standard portion of fish and chips consist of a 6oz fillet and a 6x5 bag of chips and sells for £4.75 - nice work if you can get it, eh?

In April 2008 he got a letter saying that the empty shop 150 yards up the road from him - a former convenience store had an application put in on it for A5 use as a community café. Parking was awful and he believed that his own shop would not be affected. He felt that being established for a quarter of a century would stand him in good stead with his regulars. The Local Council rejected the application, but it was over turned by the District Council and that is when his nightmare began.

Once permission was granted it wasn't long before the so-called community café was having a second hand frying range installed. Within a month it was common knowledge who was coming to town. The established operator knew he would win on quality and thought that he would have loyal customers, but he had expected the new operator to have the same approach to business as he did. However, the new operator was very different indeed. He has a very slick business plan that we should all do well to pay attention to. Taking empty sites for nil premium, fitting them out for as little as possible, selling huge portions to build turnover and then selling the sites on for huge profit has seen this new chap make a very good living - not from running fish and chip shops but from buying and selling them.

Not only that, but the new operator didn't need to register for VAT straight away as he had to reach the threshold first and this meant that he was able to slaughter the established guy on price, too. In fact the new guy even copied the old guy's colour scheme, shop layout and menu and on the first day of trade, the established frier saw his business more or less cut in half.

At this point in the story, I will let you digest what you have read. What would you do? Entering a price war would only reduce margins and leave customers wondering why you charged so much to start with. Making portions bigger again reduces margins and this type of action has to be considered an act of desperation and not a sustainable business strategy and so our luckless operator scratched his head and this is what he did…

"Good food ain't cheap and cheap food ain't good"

He decided to allow his customers to try the new business and held his nerve for the first month and took a holiday to Cornwall with his family. When he returned he entered his shop in the Fish and Chip Shop of the Year competition and sent his staff on training courses just to make sure their customer service skills were as good as they possibly could be.

BUY ONE FISH AND CHIPS GET ANOTHER ONE FREE!

He took adverts out on the local radio and in the newspapers and told his community why his fish and chips were a few pennies more. "Good food ain't cheap and cheap food ain't good", one of his mates had told him and he used that in his campaign along with all the other things he knew his competitor could not boast about, like his high efficiency pans that were environmentally friendly, his low fat fish and chips, how he sourced his fish from sustainable stocks, how his frying medium was low in trans fats and not hydrogenated, how he sponsored local football teams, employed local people and even made his own fishcakes instead of buying in cheap and nasty ones.

The new guy simply responded by doing "Buy fish and chips and get another fish and chips free!"

The credit crunch started to take hold now and although raw material costs were starting to fall, so was the number of people spending everywhere. Our established frier had never traded in an environment before where his cash reserves were actually going down. He looked at his overheads and made savings where he could without compromising on quality. He reduced his labour costs by cutting hours and managed not to let anyone go. His relationship with his bank manager had always been good - being with the same bank for thirty years since his father was in business - and not only that, in the back of his mind he knew that he had several properties in the background that were completely mortgage free and bringing in good rents. He continued to trade on quality and was slowly winning business back despite the ridiculous offers, cheaper prices and huge portions just up the road.

By now he was trading at about 75% of where his business was before the new guy had opened but then two more planning applications were passed and, before he knew it, two other takeaways had opened in quick succession and a local pub started delivering food, making 14 sites where just months before there were ten in a community of 9,000 people.

By Christmas his trade had fallen again as his customers were spoilt for choice yet again. Our established frier's cash reserves were depleted and his bank manager who had offered him an umbrella throughout their 30 year summer decided to take it away at the first sign of rain. It had become bank policy to remove managers' discretion over lending and all he could offer our guy was an expensive overdraft - despite the fact that he was extremely asset rich.

As things stand now, he no longer has that overdraft. He has released some equity from one of his properties. His success in the Fish and Chip Shop of the Year Competition has helped him a lot. He has stuck to his guns and not taken the cheap route. He stills trades on quality although he has taken the migration of his customers quite personally and feels a bit betrayed, even though it's only business at the end of the day. He believes that by protecting his margins by reducing his overheads – not his prices - and selling on quality and value was the only sustainable way to tackle the new guy who already has his shop up for sale.

> *Whoever buys this will think it's a goldmine until their realise they have paid too much for a shop that takes loads and makes nothing...*

Whoever buys it will think it's a gold mine until they realise that they have paid too much for a shop that takes loads and makes nothing. He now trades at 80% of where he was last year and he knows that it could have been far worse. If he hadn't had years of hard work behind him he knows he could have lost it all. You do not need to be a genius to figure out who this guy is and the moral of the story - well, there isn't one.

John Lennon once said "Life is what happens between making plans." I say "Life is what you make it. Your plans need to change to suit the environment you live in. Evolve or be another Woolworths."

JULY 2009 • ENERGY PROVIDERS

B ritain may have talent, but it's definitely got no flippin' common sense. If you've ever tried contacting your local environmental health department or your local planning department you'll know exactly where I'm coming from. I was so determined to get off on the right foot, I really was. I thought to myself, I'll phone and introduce my business, tell them that I was setting up a new operation and respectfully request an opportunity to meet and discuss how I could start a relationship with them on the basis that they are the law and I must be compliant.

The environmental health dude said I needed to register which seemed fairly straight forward and that I would also need to provide certain information for their approval – in particular our waste management provision and proposed extraction system. Great, I thought and so I said "Can you give me your criteria for an acceptable extraction system so that I can comply with it?"

This is where the wheels fell off the wagon…

> *I really have a problem with civil servants who flex their muscles just because they get picked on at home….*

"Oh no," he said, "we don't do that…You have to submit your system and we will approve it or tell you where it fails…" At hearing this, my blood boiled in seconds. You see, I really have a problem with civil servants who flex their muscles just because they get picked on at home. Every one knows there are hundreds of ways of doing things wrong and usually only one way (or two if you're lucky!) to do things right. What this guy was saying to me might as well have been, we know the speed limit, we're not going to tell you what it is, go as fast as you like and if we feel like it we'll arrest you.

Does it not make sense to put the horse in front of the cart? Why make us put forward a proposal when you already know what we need to do to make you happy? Why not tell us what you are looking for first and let us meet your requirements. It can't be that difficult can it?

Down the hall from the environmental health department it gets no better with the conservation officer. He is never available and the planning department are as easy to nail down as a greased eel.

I have since learnt that every local authority has its own planning criteria. That's fine. Tell me what yours is and I will comply. "Oh no, we can't do that… Central Government has the final say," says the Planning Moron. The whole process is now structured in such a way that local authorities want to see certain statements included in your application. This makes it virtually impossible for your average man to successfully complete a planning application without seeking professional help. I am convinced that it is designed to intimidate people into either not bothering in the first place or slipping up and failing.

It's all okay though because I just smiled my crocodile smile and went away. My next move is to register and jump through all the various hoops until I get what I want. It may take a year but that's fine by me too. It doesn't matter if it takes me two or three years to open because I will still probably be waiting for my new effing gas supply to be completed…

> *Getting a new gas supply is harder than pleasing the first woman you divorced*

That's right. It's not just the local authorities that have the exclusive rights on being completely useless. The gas board are quite simply in a league all by themselves. Getting a new gas supply is harder than pleasing the first woman you divorced.

First of all, only British Gas can instigate a new supply (they have loads of different contractors to do the work but you cannot speak to them). Then they hide the department you need to speak to in a telephonic abyss that takes literally days to get through, only to be

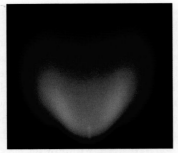

told that all operators are busy and you get thrown out again. Once you do get through, you have to apply for a quote to do the work. This application for a quote involves providing a drawing to scale with a mark on it of where you actually want the supply to go to. Once they have this, they then generate a quote (which normally means you have to sell a kidney) in about 3-4 weeks. Once you approve the quote, the contract gets allocated to a local team to do the work and this can take anywhere between 13 weeks and the rest of your life to happen.

If British Gas are in a league of their own then they will soon be joined by newly promoted Electricity Suppliers United. They cannot ever seem to read a meter correctly, charge you the correct tariff or send a bill out that corresponds to the address to which your supply relates. Don't bother phoning to complain unless you speak fairy liquid – oh, and don't ever speak to another energy provider because in their language "I am not interested" really means "Please enter me into a legally binding verbal contract and hold a gun to my head."

All is not lost though because I have been speaking to a leading Dutch range manufacturer (it just wouldn't be proper to name them) who is already exploring hydrogen technology for the next generation of frying ranges. These new ranges potentially could significantly reduce your fuel costs, produce hot clean water as a by-product and considerably reduce both your stress levels and carbon footprint.

The future's bright... the future's hydrogen....

AUGUST 2009 • VATMAN!

Before I launch into this month's column, I must respond briefly to the letter published in last month's magazine by the very liked and much respected supplier Tony Rogers. I was fortunate enough to bump into him in Leeds recently and take my medicine in person prior to FCFF going to print. I must agree that all of the points raised by Tony are indeed both extremely important and valid especially in the current economic climate.

That said however, I am a fish frier first and a diplomat second and if a fellow frier negotiates 90 days credit on their fish account and a supplier accepts those terms then I will still applaud the frier.

FISH & CHIPS - A NATIONAL TREASURE

I thank Tony for taking the time to highlight the strain that this type of arrangement could have on the supply chain and I'm sure that this type of arrangement will not be a common sight in the future. If it were common practice, I probably would not have mentioned it in the first place. In fact, I would go so far as to say that anyone who exceeds their terms should be shot and I'm sure most friers are thankful that at our end of the supply chain, we get our money back on our outlay so promptly.

I could not wait to put finger to keyboard for this month's column. Having enjoyed immensely the opportunity to vent my frustrations with civil servants and energy providers and by the way it was received by you, I can tell that most of you have all felt the pain at some time or other, I decided this month to do the VAT inspector rant as part of my continuing therapy.

You see, I have been under routine investigation by the VAT man for nearly 12 months. The year that he randomly chose to put under the spot light was 2005. So as you read this, I want you to start thinking about where you were in 2005. Now I want you to think about August 2005. Can you remember where you were living then? Of course you can. Okay, now ask yourself what vehicle you were driving then? Well done if you can remember that. I am a bit of a petrol head and change my cars like my shoes. Right then, ask yourself when you sold that vehicle and what you did with the money? If you can remember that, give yourself a gold star and go to the top of the class. If you can't remember, does it mean that you are a criminal? It does if you are VATMAN...

I am a lucky guy. My accountant charges me £80.00 a year for an insurance premium that covers any expenses in the event of a random VAT inspection. Every year, I've paid it (entered it into the books) and wondered why. This year however, having been the subject of a cavity search that left me feeling dirty and having been asked so many loaded questions that make me doubt my own innocence, I can honestly say it is the best eighty bucks that I have ever spent. To say that I have co-operated is putting it mildly. I even did a 400 mile round trip from Cornwall during a family holiday to meet VATMAN in person. Satisfied with my business dealings, he decided to pay some attention to my personal affairs and this is where VATMAN violated me almost biblically.

You see, in this country, you only have to keep personal records for 2 years and in this country if you get married, everything you receive from loved ones to help you start your new life comes via John Lewis. Before

2005 I used to sleep at night, and then my first daughter Madeleine was born. Common sense took over meaning that both the black and the silver Lotus had to go. A year before Madeleine came along, I had a Big Fat Greek wedding (you know where everyone pins cash on you) These events made my personal bank account look like a mafia dry cleaners and my bank statements and cheque stubs were eventually binned along with a tonne of nappies or buried under a mountain of soft toys.

Asking me where any sum of domestic money came from and what that sum of money went on may as well have been the questions "what aftershave was your dad wearing the day he met your mother?" and "what colour socks did he have on?" None of these events made me guilty of anything other than getting on with a busy normal life whilst running a fish and chip shop.

> *The fact that in all other aspects of law in the UK, you are presumed innocent until proven guilty doesn't matter to VATMAN*

The fact that I wanted to help, despite the fact that it was four years ago and I am not obliged to retain this information, did not stand me in any form of kind regard. The fact that culturally Greeks are different did not dent VATMAN either. The fact that in all other aspects of law in the UK, you are presumed innocent until proven guilty doesn't matter to VATMAN. No.

This super hero wears his pants under his suit. He doesn't care how much tax you've paid over the years either. He doesn't care that you have a business to run while he looks up your derriere and that trying to ruin you on an empty gut feeling, that he can no more prove than you can disprove, is likely to put 30 workers back into the benefit system bothers him not a jot. He can't see that his actions will ultimately destroy your future earning and tax paying potential and in reality kill another fertile golden goose. Oh no – he just wants an extra pound of flesh over and above the several that you have already volunteered.

Why is this? Is it because the lesser spotted tax payers are now becoming such a rare breed that those that have been regular and quiet contributors need to be squeezed into giving more? Perhaps is it that there are so many more people claiming benefits these days that makes it essential that entrepreneurs pay more taxes? Government is VATMAN's evil puppet master. A tax payer's vote is worth exactly the same as that of a benefit dosser except there's loads of them and only a few of us and so the government cuts the basic rate of VAT to win applause and votes – then sends VATMAN after soft targets to recover the shortfall. It doesn't matter to Gordon (Dark Overlord) Brown whether small businesses are still around in five years time or not because by then he knows he won't be.

Maybe to understand why VATMAN has become such a Robin Hood gone bad, we need to take a closer look at the man behind the mask. His name will almost certainly be Colin or Nigel or Rupert – he was never gonna make it as Colombo, Bergerac or Cracker. He wasn't even gonna be Inspector Clueso or Inspector Gadget for that matter. He still lives with his mum, probably, and his role is academic to him because in his head you're Ronnie Biggs and he's on to you big time. You're the reason he wears the badge and you validate his very existence. Without you, nothing makes any sense and he's gonna getchya – even if you've done absolutely nothing wrong because that's what he's paid to do. When all is over and VATMAN returns to the shadows (which has yet to happen) you may well be left feeling the same way I do...

> *His name will almost certainly be Colin or Nigel or Rupert - he was never going to make it as Colombo, Bergerac or Cracker*

I am beginning to feel like honesty is not the best policy and that crime does pay. I have seen at first hand so many businesses that simply are not as straight as me and get away with it. Uhh ohh – there we go.... Tin open.... Worms everywhere.

There seems to be little reward for ambition and nothing to gain for hard work or patriotism. It is much easier to take out of the state than put into it these days. Why should running an honest business or employing English staff make you less profitable than businesses that don't declare their takings and employ cheap foreign workers? There is such a fine line between wanting to protect one's own country and being racist that the law makers in this country are actually scared into going after easy targets rather than trying to protect them. The French and the Germans soon kick off about it – Pierre and Hans will park their lorries in ports and block motorways until the eurocrats take notice. As the pound falls in value and robbing the UK becomes less attractive to non skilled foreign cash-in-hand workers, what's going to happen then? The ones who do not go home will become self employed in cash rich businesses so they can rob more than just wages to send home.

You can expect to see even more places to get your car washed for less than a Brit will do it for and cut-price takeaways opening on every street corner from now on. They will do it for less than us and for several reasons – their takings will leave the UK and will be worth millions back home. Their workers will turn up and slog for next to nothing because it's better than being shot at back home and VATMAN will not pick on them because his real name is Derrick, he's afraid of them because they no speaka da lingo and he's too busy bustin' my balls ...

SEPTEMBER 2009 • FAREWELL MY SUMMER LOVE

Thanks to absolutely everyone last month who phoned me at 2am, in Tesco and in the mornings whilst cutting fish and on my way to dropping the kids off at school and even whilst dropping the kids off at the pool.

It seems I may have struck a bit of a chord with my VATMAN rant – so much so in fact that you contacted me in your droves to cleanse your souls and get your own painful experiences off your chests. This valuable feedback is liberating for me. It goes some way to validating my completely irrational desire to put down in black and white all the stuff that goes on between my ears. Thank you all from the heart of my bottom.

If December, January and February was our winter of discontent, then June, July and August promised to be the fish frier's opportunity to make hay while the sun shone. For this column I thought I would reflect on Summer 09 from my point of view and if you've had a different experience to me then perhaps you could pick up your pen or electronic method of communication and contact Wendy Durham – FCFF's editor. She may even publish your replies!

This year in my town, Summer arrived on a Tuesday and by Wednesday it was Autumn. I had convinced myself that the good weather was going to bring business flooding back to what had been a pretty ordinary and uninspiring spring trade – not that I'm complaining though, as other businesses around me were either moaning like injured livestock or - with almost last-breath dignity - silently slipping away to the retail park in the sky…

"…seagull-free and ever so flat…"

For generations gone by, the fish and chip trade has always had a love affair with the seaside during the summer months – leaving land-locked towns and cities behind and skipping off to the beach. Even today, a family holiday or a dirty weekend away rocking uncle Frank's caravan would not be complete without sampling the local deep fried ambrosia. Statistics said that Brits were holidaying in the UK this year and with British Airways asking their staff to work for free for a month all the signs pointed to cha-ching for seaside chippies. In my tiny little world out in the seagull-free and ever so flat fens, seventy odd miles from the coast, the same

FISH & CHIPS - A NATIONAL TREASURE   118

statistics that told us that Brits were choosing donkey rides and Punch and Judy over camel rides and punch ups with Manuel meant very little - they also claimed that fish and chip sales were well up on previous years, probably due to its perceived value for money and for all of you chip shop owners with sand in your pants, I hope you really took some coin because I didn't...

It was much better than I expected - though not because I was swamped with customers. This summer my salvation didn't arrive in the form of bumper sales, it came from amazingly cheap raw materials.

When the credit crunch kicked in and the global banking system nearly ended western civilisation, there was only so much fish around at the time and prices were much much firmer than they have been. Iceland (the country – not where mums go to bump into Kerry Katona) had a full-scale banking melt down and seeing as 99% of their gross national income is derived from fishing, they decided to get themselves out of trouble by sticking two fingers up to Brussels and increasing their fishing quotas. Months later as more and more fish hit our shores, merchants were able to replace their stock for less money and sold their expensive-to-purchase stock for less than they paid for it safe in the knowledge that they were getting new stock for eff all. Prices kept falling and we never complained.

A new bumper harvest of spuds saw their prices tumble and I'm sure that most of us (me completely, totally and utterly included) made one very simple and honest mistake that could have dramatically improved the fortunes of us fish and chip shop owners more or less overnight and possibly given us the Summer we'd all been praying for. Instead, though, we all took the extra profit from having cheap spuds and fish and said thank you very much. We took the money and ran.

You see, away from the ever so glamorous world of being a flimsy fish frying celebrity, I am a very ordinary operator with a very typical workload and stuff to get done every day. I cut fish, I peel spuds, I have staff let me down (daily) and I fry food and serve my customers. I also have to buy stock, protect my margins and set my prices. I am consumed by my job, I am sucked into it and as such I live my life as a fish frier and very rarely do I live my life as a customer. As I was going about my business this summer, things were changing on the other side of the counter and I missed it (along with loads of other friers) until it was too late.

Since late spring, some smart retailers had begun to realize that although businesses were being starved of cash flow in the high street, the public were enjoying low interest rates and actually had money, but were being cautious about spending it. Fear of job insecurity and the value of people's homes falling made everyone look hard at where they spent their hard earned pennies. Big high street names were going to the wall and Mr or Mrs Average Joe stopped trusting slick adverts and started trusting price. The honest reality was that to get them to part with their money in Summer 2009 you had to make their pennies go further.

We had the margins in our low raw material costs, our low interest rates and fantastic cash flow to offer fish and chips for far less than we had for years and years - and yet we all did nothing. Imagine how busy you would have been throughout July and August if your chips were down to just fifty pence a portion - with every fish purchased. It wouldn't have hurt you to do it because the margins on your fish were so damn good in July and August you would have been no worse off than in spring on margins, but up on sales by a country mile. Let's face it, if your spud bill went up a hundred pounds a week but you were selling an extra 100 kilos of cod a week – you wouldn't be exactly crying about it, would you? Deals on meals - even now - is where the long queues are but be quick because prices are starting to climb again. Be cute - and don't devalue your product at the same time. When you reduce your price, remember to tell your customers what a great deal it is and how long it will go on for and most importantly why you have decided to do it.

Not all of us missed the boat but so many did. The opportunity to build my own cash reserves was just too much for me to resist. All is not lost though because in my next column I am going to write about our menu boards and why they are hurting our business so badly. If you take my advice (which incidentally was taught to me by my extremely talented manager Ian Kilby) and make some subtle changes to the way you sell your meals, you might just have to buy me a drink the next time you see me...

November 2009 • Menu therapy

It's blacker than the inside of a coffin on a moonless night when you get up in the morning these days and if you're a frozen-at-sea fish cutter like me, defrosting your hands takes as long as it does to be able to see out of your windscreen before you start your journey to work.

That means it's November and if your shop is well illuminated, it should look as inviting on these dark winter nights to a hungry customer as the playboy mansion would to a monk with a weekend pass from the good lord himself.

Instead of venting this month, my therapist has asked me to turn the tables and put you on my couch. In my last column I said I would talk about menu boards – in particular how we do them in our fish and chip shops and why I think we've got it all wrong. So relax, breath deeply and listen to the sound of my words...

Ask any of our trade bodies how to properly promote our products and we will all get a bog standard recipe for success – rows of menu items, accurately describing, without misleading or falling foul of any trade description rules, each individual delight with a price neatly placed in the opposite row. An example might be "Whole tail scampi......£3.00". Another might be "Regular cod......£3.25" and so on and so on.

For years and years and years we have all pretty much followed this format - some of us use black boards and chalk, some use illuminated boxes with stick-on letters (which us friers replace with wonky ones when we put our prices up!) and some of us have even gone to great lengths and expense to pay for a photo of some fish and chips that looks nothing like the meal we sell in our shops. For all those customers who had forgotton what laboratory fish and chips cooked in the 1980's looks like, we also marry those clinical images to a high tech illuminated menu system where we slot into place slides that describe the meal and price. They are great because they are easily changeable - if you can remember where you put the spares and if you have enough left over 5's when you want to put prices up a few pence.

So what's wrong with that? The short answer is that we are harming ourselves by displaying our prices this way. Last month I made comment about how we get sucked into our business. We analyse it, we pour so much of our energy into it and we want it to be a success but do we take the time to be a customer in our own shops? Do we look at their experience? Do we consider what a visit to our shop must be like? Most of us don't - but we are customers elsewhere so let me ask you a few questions that you should be able to answer correctly. How much does a Big Mac cost on its own? How much is a chicken madras with a pilau rice from your local Indian takeaway? When was the last time you paid an extra charge for a pizza because you spent less than the minimum amount required to qualify for free delivery?

The problem is that WE make price THE BIG ISSUE in our shops. We confront our customers with our prices. Before they have made their selection, we have reminded them how much everything is and reduced the feel good factor they would get from treating themselves to fish and chips, making them less likely to deviate into purchasing anything more than they need.

Our competitors hide the price on their menus in their stores. The multiples are the best at it. Their menus are designed to help you purchase high margin extras you don't even want, like fries and a soft drink. You buy a meal deal – not because you are more hungry or thirsty than when you visit a chippy or because it represents better value than buying them separately, but because that is what you are presented with when you look up at the board for guidance. The member of staff then adds further insult by persuading you into going large for a few pennies more. You would need to hold a gun to spotty boy's head to get him to sell you just a burger and even then you forget about the price because you've already decided that it is what you want before you are presented with the bill.

In other outlets like ethnic or pizza stores they don't put prices on the all. They list them in military fashion and make you search through nearly a hundred different items to find the one you are looking for and

when you do, because it is a similar price as a number 68 or a number 79, you do not consider it expensive, although all of it really, really is. When you look at how your competition sells its food, it makes you wonder whether they are damaging your business or are we doing it to ourselves?

...time to start enticing them by making them want the food before they think about the cost...

Next time you re-do your menu, think about it. It's time to stop educating our customers by making them think about every penny and time to start enticing them by making them want the food before they think about the cost. Try promoting meals instead of individual items – include peas, curry or a can of pop with the meal and use images of your own food so that folk can see really what they will get for their money. It takes away the need to physically beat your staff into trying to upsell extras to customers. It helps customers decide what to buy and helps you to influence your customers' spend in a positive way. High margin items like peas, curry sauce and cans of fizzy pop boost takings and profits as well as adding real value to a customers decision to visit your store. Take down your prices and put your price list on the back of the door so they can see it as they leave. Get your offers and fantastic specials that you want to sell in front of the customer.

Most importantly, it is absolutely vital that you buy me a drink the next time you see me with the extra few quid you've got in your pocket.

....and as I count down from ten you're back in the room, eyes open, wide awake.

APRIL 2010 • MICROCHIPS AND FISHY BUSINESS

I am off the soapbox and back into the chipbox again this month. Although my comments may have been abrasive to some, I don't think anyone can argue just how timely it was in the face of recent events that followed its publication. Now staring at a future sans Seafish, the thought of them not being around to promote our brand or police the training of our future generation of friers must leave many (including me) thankful that we still have the NFFF who are not government funded, or subsidised by anything other than membership fees to continue providing the important support they have been doing for nearly a hundred years.

I am going to share with you all this month an exciting and new technique for strengthening relationships with your customers and why embracing this new opportunity is so right now and so well suited to fish and chip shops and even more of a good opportunity for established operators to use in the fight against brand new competition.

In the white collar world of marketing, large organisations are booking their young dynamic Porsche driving executives onto seminars and one day courses to learn about the new buzz world of social networking. It started with "Friends Reunited" a flawed website where successful people could see how ordinary the people they didn't like at school ended up. The creator sold it to ITV and bought a small country near the Mediterranean and ITV cried its eyes out when they tried to charge everyone a fiver to use it and it died on its feet.

MSN became the new playground because kids whose parents were smart enough to not let them have mobile phones (and it's getting less and less) could log on and have instant conversations about who kissed who behind the bike sheds without it costing a penny and even better, parents thought they were doing their home work. MSN still has a following but it also fell foul of two brand new online communities that have simply taken the art of conversation and communication from being a physical act and shredded the fabric of society by dissolving it into a cyber matrix. There are now three realities that you have to get your head round and accept quickly here. The first reality is that social clubs, pubs and living breathing congregations will eventually be on the endangered species list – occupied only by people who do not get on the technology bus. The second reality is that online opportunities available now to stay in touch with loved ones are actually much faster, more convenient and even easier for people with even the most basic of

computer skills to use than picking up the phone and getting caught in a conversation you don't actually want to have. Finally, the third reality is that it is so cost effective and already so bloody simple to reach so many people that to ignore its potential puts you behind everyone else who is on board right now.

I am a complete numpty when it comes to computers. I can't even upload a picture or download an MP3 without the help of my five year old daughter. It's true though that I did recognise the need for an online community for fish friers five years ago and paid someone with the skills to make it a reality. Chippychat is a specialist site that services a particular group of individuals and it does it very well and it has proven to be a valuable asset to our trade - but I am not talking about Chippychat today.

I am talking about Facebook and Twitter. You see these sites have attracted squillions and gargillions of followers who are already your customers. The whole of the world has stopped phoning and writing to loved ones and friends. Petrol and diesel prices have made it too expensive to actually go and visit them – plus you might catch swine flu if you share the same air as them anyway. You can now stay in your underpants, not put your face on and still see what they've been up to because every one now posts photos and updates of everything they've been up to. You simply accept a friend request or ask someone you know to be your friend and quickly build up a portfolio of folk that you want to follow and share your news with. You may not want to know about their latest bowel movement but it will be on there at some point – guaranteed.

Now explore the potential for an established shop versus a new kid on the block. If you can get your customers to become your friend, then you can ask their friends to become your friend too. You can tell them about any promotional activity you might want to engage in. You can do give-aways and exclusive offers to your friends and make friendship a valuable thing for your customers to be a part of. You can get feedback from them too and most importantly, you can show your personal side with status updates that are not geared towards selling at all – in fact it

is my policy to only use a sales message in one out of every four posts I make. If you become a pest rather than someone your friends can connect with and relate to, you become a nuisance and clutter their important social interaction.

Last month, I gave away a free meal to anyone who could predict the England v Egypt final score before the half-time whistle blew. I raffled a 4.5 kilo Easter egg, dropped the price of my thick-shakes to 50p for Facebook chums only and also warned my 750 friends when a copper was hiding up the road with a speed trap gun. The whole lot cost me less than a hundred bucks and made me a real popular fellow. Now imagine opening a new business in a new town, placing a £500 ad in the local paper and wondering where all the people are?

The fish and chip industry has always been the envy of multiple operators because we are all part of a network of independents. We each have the ability to be flexible enough to adapt our products and services to exceed the individual needs and expectations of every single customer we have. The big chains need rigid formulas that must be adhered to in order to deliver consistent service and products at a price that allows them to make a profit and meet their customers' expectations. Our flexibility can be exploited even more on social networking sites because the big chains cannot interact on such a human level. They have an image and a brand but no personality or presence inside their customers own lives.

Without financial restraint, we are now able to boldly go where no burger chain has gone before…

CHAPTER SEVEN - DO TRY THIS AT HOME

So, you've read six chapters and now you're starting to get hungry – right? Well I am not about to unlock the mystic secrets of the frying art for the price of a paperback book.

Being a master frier is as individual as a snowflake. I can teach you how I do it for about a thousand pounds. All you will need is a shop and a frying range and an open mind. I don't do domestic – even I don't cook fish and chips at home (unless you're my brother in law or my bank manager) – it's dangerous and unless you're a pro, it won't be as good as when we do it, or as cheap. Supermarkets charge more for raw fish than we do for it fried to perfection.

I have decided, though, that in true celebrity chef style (who am I trying to kid?) I must have recipes in this book and so here are some that I think work, as they go well with the meal that I am celebrating in these pages.

But why take over a fortnight to crawl a week - when you can run there in a day? My recipes are in keeping with the whole spirit of what fish and chips is about. No pretentious pollocks! Just stripped down easy recipes that work. The reality is you probably won't bother to try these out, but if you do, you will get really great results.

If you want to impress someone special in your life without breaking the bank or the kitchen, now you can make a meal of it without making a meal of it. All these extras are designed to add a personal touch to your weekly trip to the chippy. Just leave the experts to handle the main course!

FISH CAKES

Ingredients

400g cod fillet (or 200g of white fish and 200g of salmon or smoked haddock etc.)

2 large potatoes - 400g (Maris Piper is good because it is not too floury or waxy – choose a different variety to give a different texture or bite)

40g butter

Salt and freshly ground black pepper

½ pack dried parsley.

Method

1 Cover the cod with cling film in a bowl with a tablespoon of water and nuke in the microwave for 2 minutes until the fish starts to flake. Allow to cool.

2 Boil the potatoes until they offer no resistance to a fork. Drain well and mash until smooth. Beat in the butter (or even better – use left over mashed potato from the meal before). Allow to cool and bind.

3 Flake the fish into pieces and twist into the potato – the more you mix the smoother the fishcake will be (I like to be able to feel the fish in mine), over season to taste (I find it absorbs into the mix and can get lost in the frying process). Add the parsley earlier if you want green fishcakes but I prefer to add them last.

4 Divide the mixture into 8 and shape into ovals about 2.5cm thick. Cover and chill for 30 minutes or until required. Chilling them is important as it binds the ingredients and stops them from breaking up when cooked - they can be cooked from frozen.

5 Crumb them by using an off the shelf crumb or by making a crumb from bread that has been dried in the oven and bashed up. Make the crumb stick by dipping the fishcake into a batter made from flour and water. Deep fry or pan fry or bake with a little spray of oil.

CHIP SHOP MUSHY PEAS

Ingredients
Dried marrowfat peas
Bicarbonate of soda
Salt and sugar

Method
1 Place the peas into a large saucepan, with enough space to allow them to more than triple in size. Cover with water by at least an inch and stir in a tea spoon of bicarbonate of soda for every 2 cups of peas. Leave to soak over night (the bicarb breaks down the outer shell of the peas and soften them prior to cooking.)
2 After soaking overnight, drain the peas and rinse well – visually inspect the peas for impurities like small stones.
3 Place the peas back into the generous sized saucepan and just cover with hot tap water. Place on a high heat and bring up to the boil. Once boiling, reduce the heat and simmer for 40 minutes, stirring regularly and adding water if necessary– do not allow the peas to re-boil as they may harden. Season with salt and sugar to your taste.
Mushy peas freeze well and when added to left over mashed potato and pressed into patties, make great mushy pea fritters.

TARTARE SAUCE

Ingredients
8 fl oz (225 ml) of thick mayonnaise
1 tbsp of chopped gherkins
1 tbsp of chopped capers (alternatively swap gherkins and capers for gherkin relish)
1 tbsp of lemon juice
1 tbsp of freshly chopped chives
1 tbsp of freshly chopped parsley
salt and pepper

Method
1 Chop ingredients into small pieces.
2 Place all of the ingredients together into a mixing bowl and combine thoroughly with a spoon or spatula.
3 Check the seasoning and adjust if necessary.
4 Cover the bowl with a layer of cling film and refrigerate for at least 30 minutes before serving.

CHIP SHOP CURRY SAUCE

Ingredients:
1 onion and 1 apple (and sultanas if desired)
1 tbsp curry powder
2 tbsp rapeseed oil
2 tbsp plain flour
400 ml water (2/3 pint)
1 tbsp tomato purée
Lemon juice to taste
Salt and pepper to taste

Method
1 Chop the onion and apple and fry on a medium heat with the curry powder in the oil until tender.
2 Sprinkle in the flour and stir in well to make a paste, cook for 2 minutes and then remove from the heat before it starts to thicken and add the water and tomato purée stirring constantly. Return to the heat and simmer for 5-10 minutes until thick. Add salt, pepper and lemon juice to taste.

FRITTERS/ BATTER RECIPES

If you really must open fry at home, then I guess I ought to give you a few ideas and point you in the right direction. Over the years and miles, I have come across some weird and wonderful offerings in batter. The most common of these items are advertised as a "fritter" or "battered".

The first group that needs to be dealt with is chocolate – Mars bars being the most famous, although I can confirm that creme eggs are also particularly scrummy. I don't do them in my shop and to be perfectly honest, I don't like frying them either – they can impart a flavour into your oil if you don't time it to perfection and in my opinion they produce a taste experience that I would describe as a sickly molten magma. If you are trying these at home – you have several challenges. The first is making the batter stick to the chocolate. I recommend either scoring a very dry chocolate bar to create something for the batter to cling to or warming it up to make it sticky and then flouring the outside of the chocolate bar prior to battering it.

Either way, your next challenge is frying the damn thing. Your batter needs to be thick enough to coat the chocolate and thin enough to cook before the chocolate melts in the pan. The key is once the batter is cooked you need to get the product out of your pan and let the heat of the batter warm the chocolate. Leave it too long and it gets messy and dangerous.

Sausages, pineapple rings, spam, corned beef, burgers, potato scallops, mushrooms, baked beans, mushy peas and even chips are regularly being served up today fried in batter. My bullet-proof batter recipe has always been self raising flour and cold water. Nothing else. Mixed for at least a minute and a half to get enough lift into it and rested for a quarter of an hour minimum. It needs to cling to your finger for a moment and then run off the finger in a continuous trail like a rats tail. If it holds too long or runs in drips, it is too thick. If you can see your finger through it and it doesn't cling, it is too thin. You can add a pale ale or lager to this for an authentic beer batter, use sparkling water for a lighter tempura style batter or add some vinegar or salt or secret ingredient if you want to be a ponce.

That's it - no more help from me because this is how I make my living and I really *don't* want you to try this at home...

CHAPTER EIGHT – THE FUTURE OF FISH AND CHIPS...

So what's next for our Dynamic Duo? In the first 150 years, we've seen a product that's changed very little in its preparation, production or consumption. It simply never needed fixing because it was never broken. It's had its critics – mostly those who want to cash in on the revenue stream that is a by-product of the love affair we have with fish and chips. When these spin doctors served up their toxic potions to discourage Great Britain – fish friers responded with silence – not from choice, but because of lack of unity and resources. We got away with saying nothing simply because the honesty of the dish itself was strong enough to see the competition and the bad news stories off.

Technology and innovation helped fish and chips to "slim down" over a decade ago, making it probably one of the healthiest takeaway meals available today and we need the public to know about it. But we don't have the expertise or the funds to tell them. Across the board, as an industry, we are using fish from monitored stocks and introducing our customers to new species all the time to ensure there will always be "plenty more fish in the sea." Potatoes should always be around although varieties may come and go. Flour and water are not under threat and as long as the motor vehicle industry carries on developing hydrogen technology and stops cutting down the rain forests, we should all still be able to source a suitable, sustainable frying medium in which to produce the dish itself.

> *...fish and chips prevails as a source of nourishment, comfort and affordable food for the masses*

And so with the question of the long term viability of raw materials addressed, I am fairly confident that as long as there is a civilised western culture (some may already question the existence of one) – there will always be a place for fish and chips in it. Today, as in days gone by, fish and chips prevails as a source of nourishment, comfort and affordable food for the masses – replacing extravagant fine dining as a trendy way to spend an evening without the chore of cooking. Staying in has become the "new" going out! The Winter of 2009/2010 has been as hard and as harsh for some individuals and businesses as the recovery after the Second World War

and when Winston Churchill described fish and chips as "the good companions", he might have summed up perfectly how the country has turned to fish and chips again, with sales increasing against the trends of other meals. As we enter the Teenies, the High Street is in utter turmoil. The country is on its knees and the mood of the nation is lower than a snake's belly.

Big name brands have folded and one National Institution that has fared far worse that the local chippy is of course the boozer - the rub-a-dub-dub - the watering hole or more commonly known - the pub. Breweries have evolved and nowadays attempt to make as much money from being landlords as they do from turning cereal crops into falling-down water.

Managed houses are in big trouble. In better times, breweries borrowed money to grow the number of sites they owned so that they could sell more beer at inflated prices. They serviced the money they borrowed by charging tenants rent and through controlled beer prices - leaving just enough margin in the wet sales to create a reasonable living for the operator - if they kept sales high enough. When the economy went to pot however, people couldn't afford to go out drinking any more and supermarket giants with huge purchasing power offered the same brands of alcohol for home consumption at a fraction of the price that the breweries (who made the stuff) were prepared to sell to their pub tenants.

The breweries believed that the going out and drinking experience added value and so, instead of addressing the problem, they put up rents and beer prices to meet the shortfall in sales. This took most tenants past breaking point as they could not sell their products at a price that allowed them to make a living and this caused pubs to close at the phenomenal rate of more than 10 sites a day around the UK.

Free houses did little better than tied ones and this was again mainly due to supermarket prices plus a quite over-looked influence in the form of improved home entertainment systems. The emergence of games consoles and an explosive advancement in television and internet based services simply meant that folk just stopped going out…

This sorry state of affairs, along with decades of diversification and subsequent saturation of our high streets with food offer after food offer after takeaway after takeaway after hairdressers leads me to make my first prediction for fish and chips for the next 150 years...

Fish and chip shops may well do better to depart from our High Streets to take up a more sustainable future as the Champion Salvation of the Great British Pub.

Think about it. It makes complete sense. It's a jolly noble and British thing to do as well. Fish and chips does not deserve to be compared to Subway or McDonalds or any other type of junk fast food. It would be more insulting to me than comparing the Queen to Madonna. The dish itself is best served straight away – we know that - but if you do want to take it home then why not get a jar down your neck and chat to old Frank while you wait for it to be fried to perfection and wrapped up? Pubs deserve to be saved. They are almost as important a part of our history as fish and chips (let's not go that far!) in that they celebrate something worth holding on to. It's called Britishness – like men with onions, stripy shirts and berets called Pierre who ride a bike make France French. British pubs have been doing fish and chips for yonks but ain't it rubbish compared to the proper stuff?

In the future, empty boozers should have frying ranges fitted and if we're really, really lucky become fish and chip emporiums which become once again the hub of every community and a place to enjoy good company, great food  and still have change for bus fare home.

Fish and chips has in more recent times been associated with the aging population – so much so that I myself wrote an article about it for Fish & Chips and Fast Food magazine and questioned then whether we were sitting, not on a time bomb, but more on a poisonous gas canister that has a progressively leaky valve. The conclusion I came to then, and I still stand by it today, is that really appreciating fish and chips is very much like finding faith or losing the ability to dance to contemporary music – it comes later in life when you allow yourself to take the time to harvest the fruits of your labour. One of the challenges for the future, then, appears to be how do we "sex up" fish and chips and make it appeal to younger generations as well as every passing one?

Having considered this and discussed it with my cyber network of fellow friers on chippychat.co.uk, I want to make several observations about a few of the things that haven't been tried yet.

To my knowledge, no one has yet managed to fund a sustained television campaign for the generic brand of fish and chips. (Save for the brilliant Friars Pride who did it locally once, back in the eighties.) Imagine where the brand of fish and chips would be if it had the weight of a national advertising budget? If the general public actually knew how this honest, virtuous and skillfully crafted dish was delivered to their plates for so little cost – then they would surely have to concede what a superb value meal they were getting? It really is champagne food at lemonade prices.

If we were to follow the cola companies and employ the services of the last singing sensation, sporting athlete or movie heart throb – then who would be able to resist the "meal for the next generation!"?

One of a whole new generation of fish and chip lovers tucks in to a Magpie takeaway in Whitby. *Photograph by kind permission of Victoria Wallop*

And what if we were to ditch our own individual identities in favour of a likeable cheeky character that the kids will love?

All of these promotional activities and techniques have been used successfully - to the detriment of fish and chips - even though the products they were actually trying to sell were rubbish. They would work even better if we used them to sell honest, natural food. It naturally follows then that we can perform this type of activity in the future with a clear conscience safe in the knowledge that we have the moral high ground.

Finally, why the heck haven't we launched a Pollock Korma, Haddock Chow Mein or even pushed the fish butty in a seeded bap with fries and a soft drink? At the very least we could have tried selling smaller sized portions of fish in a 1, 2 or 3 piece dinner format with side orders in a bargain bucket.

Looking forward let's consider also what is happening today that may hint as to the direction of the meal itself? Before I do, though, I have a confession to make. When I was a young man full of opinion but low in depth of character and knowledge of the trade, I was fortunate enough to reach the final of the Drywite Young Fish Frier of the Year competition. I was asked in the final judging round how I saw the future of fish and chips and my response then cost me dearly. I was of the opinion back in 1986 that the emerging generation of fish and chip lovers would not appreciate the taste or benefits of freshly prepared chipped potatoes and that because their mums fed them frozen, pre-packed, reformed chips, they would be likely to expect their local chippy to deliver the same rubberised incarnation or suffer as a result.

Thankfully the wheels of time proved the judges correct when they dismissed my theories and awarded the title to someone else. (Duncan

Nash) I will not make the same mistake again, but I will go so far as to say that the on-site daily production of fresh cut chipped potatoes is under threat. Capital expenditure, the cost of water along with labour rates and consistency and space issues are forcing more and more friers to explore the convenience of a sub-contracted supply of ready prepared, fresh-cut chipped potatoes. We will still however stick with the real thing whether we peel it and chip it ourselves or not.

The world is covered by literally thousands upon thousands of miles of ocean with depths that man can barely comprehend. It is reasonable to assume that over the next 150 years once man has found ET, he will start to explore the potential of the seas. The tides offer so much free kinetic energy that globally, plans are already well under way to harness the power of waves as clean, renewable energy. I feel confident in predicting that, unless we continue to treat our planet with absolutely no respect, our waters will continue to provide man with new and exciting opportunities. With no threat to the five basic elements of fish and chips, I have to conclude that the product itself is likely to be considered not only the original fast food but will also end up being regarded as the first of many treasures given up to man from the ocean.

If the product is going to remain unchanged, then what can we predict about the competition? There's an old saying: "There's more than one way to skin a cat". This may be very true and I don't think it will be unreasonable to consider that the big budgets and suits out there will continue to revamp, re-launch and re-invent meat, vegetables and something moist between two slices of manipulated carbohydrate, or mask some cleverly portioned cut of cheap meat with indistinguishable spices and grey matter along with coloured rice. If the High Street becomes too crowded or too expensive for fish and chips to maintain its presence then it will not die out. It will have gone up market to a place where people will be prepared to pay a price that allows the fish frier to make a profit.

There are new markets desperate to embrace fish and chips. Take New York, for example. With a footprint of over 350 square miles and a population of 88 million people, not to mention the workers and tourists that swell those numbers every single day, diverse in both culture and financial means. The Big Apple – start spreading the news - only four fish and chips shops in whole goddamn place, man. The Americans love fish and chips too. They love 'em because it connects them to a history and heritage they long for but don't have. They love us Brits too, with our crooked teeth and our quaint little accents and tight bottoms. The land of opportunity beckons – the American dream for me would be to go over there and do to Uncle Sam what Ronald McDonald failed to do to Blighty. Thank goodness the guy was a clown.

In fact, anywhere the British Empire left its mark or its language is fair game. We are far too lazy to learn another language but the Aussies or the Canadians (the English speaking ones, anyway) would totally love fish and chips. Let's not forget our Euro partners in Spain, Greece and Portugal who sold time share villas to our parents, and don't dismiss the Russians either - they catch cod and fell in love with fish and chips when they came over and satisfied our manual labour needs.

So let me wrap this thing up good and proper then, without salt or vinegar. What I can predict about the future of fish and chips is this. They will definitely be around for the foreseeable future with no immediate or predictable environmental or ethical threats. The meal

Photo courtesy Asntruther Fish Bar

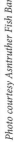

itself will be virtually unchanged in composition, although presentation may improve and I expect more innovations in frying technology to arrive that will make it virtually fat free. Frying equipment will almost certainly end up being powered by hydrogen, producing as a by-product all the hot water a discerning operator needs to keep his premises spotlessly clean.

If the Network of Independent Retailers get their act together as a united marketing force, and learn to promote the product, it will continue as the Number One meal and its popularity will go global. Expect to see strong chains of shops emerge to power this branding revolution with probably two or three front-runners taking the lead. If as an industry we fail to unite to promote and protect, we will end up declining in numbers, although the strong shops will always survive and there will always be a following.

Whatever happens, fish and chips will still continue to represent a transparent, honest, value for money meal when compared to all other pretenders or challengers - and that's good enough for me.

INDEX